GONE

FISHING

GONE FISHING

MIKKEL KARSTAD

Photography
Anders Schønnemann

GOING FISHING

I still remember my first great fishing expedition. I was in Greenland with my father and his wife where we helped a shepherd build his new sheep farm. The farm was situated right on the shores of a very beautiful and rocky fjord, surrounded by breathtakingly beautiful landscape.

One day, a couple of Danish boys and I walked down to the fjord. We hadn't brought much fishing gear, just a hand line and spoon bait, which we threw out as far as we could. This was no more than 10-15 metres, but on our second attempt, we caught a gigantic cod (well maybe it wasn't exactly gigantic). To a six-year-old boy it was a huge fish and the experience left a lasting impression.

For the rest of that day, and indeed the remaining time we spent in Greenland, we caught a lot of fish: cod, sea scorpions, halibut and perfect wild salmon from the teeming river. We ate nothing but fish for an entire month, and it tasted absolutely wonderful. But I do remember that the last meal we had, before returning to Denmark, was lamb and potatoes. Never before had a simple dish with lamb and large boiled potatoes tasted so good. But even then I was seriously hooked on fish.

Seafood remained important as I was growing up – I spent summer holidays on the Danish island of Anholt, where I worked on the docks, helping local fishermen pull sole and edible crabs from their nets. I'd spend the afternoons catching weever fish off the pier with only a small float and shrimps as bait. I still remember my record catch of 41 weevers in one afternoon. I accidentally pricked my hand on the poisonous spikes of the very first one I caught, but I refused to go home even though I felt slightly queasy.

I also spent numerous holidays with my family in Tåsinge, a small peninsular in Southern Funen, where my uncle set traps and we caught hundreds of eels. Early mornings were spent wading through warm shallow water to sweep fjord shrimps, my cousins and I catching shore crabs with our crab-strings in the little local harbour. And most of it would eventually be included in a meal later in the day: fried eel with new potatoes, parsley sauce and pickled cucumber; freshly peeled fjord shrimps on toast with homemade mayonnaise; and stone crab soup – so simple and so good!

When I started my chef's training, I listed 10 restaurants in Copenhagen where I wanted to work. At the top of that list was Krog's Fish Restaurant, due to its amazing reputation and because, back then,it was the best seafood restaurant in town and thus a completely natural place for me to do my training. I was lucky when they took me on. I worked there for four years and learned even more about seafood and how to prepare it than I had growing up.

In the last few years I haven't been fishing as much as I would've liked to. And unfortunately, I haven't had time to pass all my knowledge on to my children, despite the fact it was a natural part of my own upbringing. However, when my family and I spent three weeks in the summer on the US West Coast, we had both the time and opportunity. I taught them how to catch crabs with their bare hands and beautiful trout with light fishing gear in the Wilson River, as well as Dungeness Crabs, Gaper Clams and wild oysters in Netarts Bay. Then we'd barbecue everything we'd caught at the hut we stayed in. Noting the fun we all had and having felt the pride that swelled up in me as I watched my children catch, handle and eat all the lovely things we fished out of river and sea, I decided that fishing, as well as gathering and eating seafood, would become a more prominent part of our everyday lives.

Seafood has always been a favourite of mine. I love preparing and eating seafood, but I also take great pride in teaching others how to eat and prepare seafood. I just want to show people how easy, simple and straightforward serving seafood actually is, and what the endless possibilities for experimentation are.

The waters of the North Sea and Atlantic Ocean are full of delicious seafood, and yet we only ever eat five different types of fish. So this book is written to inspire us to choose from a much wider selection than many people realize is available, and to develop new ways of preparing and eating them.

You can catch or gather all the different types of seafood mentioned in this book in the waters surrounding Northern Europe or the Atlantic, in their lakes and in their rivers. Or you could simply ask your local fishmonger to order some as they all have access to these fish, just not enough demand … There is no excuse, simply tuck into some lovely seafood.

Plaice in newspaper 18 · Twistbread with asparagus and dog roses 21 · Hot-smoked eel on a BBQ starter with hay and embers 24 ·
Shore crab bisque with sweet corn, fried cabbage and tarragon 29 · Crunchy cookies with dried blueberries and spelt flakes 30

FROM THE
SEA

PLAICE WRAPPED IN NEWSPAPER

4 PEOPLE

—————

4 whole plaice with skin on

a handful of seaweed or herbs, such as
   dill, fennel, thyme

salt

1–2 newspapers

Spread the newspapers out on a flat surface. Spread the seaweed over the paper and position the plaice on top before sprinkling it with salt. Wrap the plaice well in both seaweed and newspaper. Sprinkle water on the newspaper until it's wet through. Wrap the remaining three plaice in the same manner before placing them in the fire.

You should only put two plaice in the fire at one time, as the fire may otherwise lose too much heat. You can put more firewood on top of the newspaper wrappings, to make sure that the plaice are cooked through. Cook the plaice for approx. 15 minutes, or until the newspaper is dried out and starting to char on the outside.

Take the packages from the fire and unwrap the plaice. Scrape off their skin and serve them straight away, while still hot. Serve with asparagus twists and a crisp green salad.

TWISTBREAD

WITH ASPARAGUS AND DOG ROSES

4 PEOPLE

8 green asparagus

1 handful dog (wild) roses
  (you can also use rose petals that
  have not been sprayed, dandelion or
  elderflowers instead)

1 portion twistbread dough

4-8 sticks to wrap the twistbread
  dough around

salt

a little olive oil

15 g yeast

300 ml water

100 ml beer

1 tbsp. olive oil

600 g organic wheat flour

a little salt

Break off the ends of the asparagus before rinsing them in cold water. Place an asparagus alongside one of the sticks and twist the dough around it. Make sure you include some dog rose petals while twisting the dough around the stick.

Continue this procedure until all asparagus and dough is used up and then bake them over the fire until golden on the outside and baked all the way through, ensuring that the asparagus have also been cooked, yet remain crispy. Sprinkle with a little salt and possibly some olive oil. Serve the twistbreads with the plaice wrapped in newspaper.

You can also make asparagus rolls at home, baking them in a conventional oven at 200° C for 12-15 minutes.

TWISTBREAD DOUGH

Dissolve the yeast in water and beer before adding olive oil and a little flour. Then add salt and the rest of the flour and knead until the dough is firm and supple. Leave the dough to rise for approx. one hour in a warm place, before making the twistbreads. You might want to start this process at home, bringing the risen dough with you in a container to the beach.

HOT SMOKED EEL

USING A BARBECUE CHIMNEY STARTER WITH HAY AND WOODFIRE EMBERS

4 PEOPLE

2 eels

a little salt

1 barbecue chimney starter

hay and woodfire embers

1 bunch of chives, preferably with flowers

2 pasteurized egg yolks

1 tbsp. mustard

1 tbsp. cider vinegar

1 tsp. salt

freshly ground pepper

150 ml rape- or grape seed oil

Skin the eels and clean out blood and intestines. Rinse well in cold water. Sprinkle a little salt on top and let them rest for 15–20 minutes.

Put some hay in the barbecue starter and place a burning log (from the camp or beachfire you've already lit) on top. Turn the barbecue starter on its head. Place the eels on the 'bottom grid' allowing the smoke and heat to enclose the eels.

Smoke the eels for approx. 10 minutes. The smoke and heat from the embers will ensure that they are cooked. Remove the eels from the barbecue starter and serve in smaller pieces with chive mayonnaise and chive flowers.

CHIVE MAYONNAISE

Add chives, egg yolks, mustard, vinegar, salt and pepper to a bowl and beat with a hand whisk until it becomes a thick egg cream. Then add the oil slowly while whisking, to make sure the mayonnaise doesn't separate. Once you've added all the oil, add a little salt and pepper to taste, possibly also a little more vinegar. Serve the mayonnaise with the hot-smoked eels. This mayonnaise is also good in open sandwiches, especially egg ones.

Tip: Barbecue chimney starters are simple aluminized steel containers with handles, which are used to start barbecues and help to heat charcoal quickly. See image on p23 for my vintage version! They're inexpensive and easily available online and offline.

Shore crab bisque with sweetcorn, fried cabbage and tarragon

SHORE CRAB (EUROPEAN GREEN CRAB) BISQUE

WITH SWEET CORN, FRIED CABBAGE AND TARRAGON

4 PEOPLE

1 kg live shore crabs
   (1kg is about 20-25 crabs)
500 ml rapeseed oil
2 onions
2 cloves garlic
1 carrot
2 fresh tomatoes
5 thyme sprigs
100 ml apple juice
330 ml wheat beer
1½ – 2 litres water
salt, sugar, vinegar and freshly
   ground pepper
one old cast-iron pot
2 corn on the cob
¼ pointed cabbage
tarragon

Shore crabs are very suitable for soup dishes, for in spite of having no meat on them, their shells add terrific flavour .
Kill the crabs by cutting them lengthwise with a strong knife. Place each crab on its back, on a chopping board, or a large flat stone if you're on the beach. Keep it still by pressing a knife blade against its breastplate. Then press so hard, you cut through its head. Repeat until there are no more crabs left and scrape crabs and juices into a bowl as you work.

Place the pot on a fire and allow it to get really hot. Roast the crabs in oil alongside the rinsed vegetables and thyme sprigs, until they're well done. Add apple juice and beer and let it simmer and reduce to half. Then add water until the crabs are just covered before adding herbs and bringing it all to the boil.

Let the soup simmer vigorously for 20 minutes. Then strain it and reduce the liquid a little more. Add salt, sugar, cider vinegar and freshly ground pepper to taste.

Slice the corn kernels vertically off the cobs and cut the cabbage into smaller chunks. Serve the soup while it's hot with raw sweet corn, cabbage and a little chopped tarragon on top. Along with good bread this is a wonderfully simple and tasty dish.

CRISP COOKIES

WITH DRIED BLUEBERRIES AND SPELT FLAKES

4 PEOPLE

160 g spelt flakes

140 g wheat flour

150 g icing sugar

225 g soft butter

a little salt

1 egg

3-4 tbsp. dried blueberries

Place all ingredients in a magimix and blend, or in a bowl and mix well with a wooden spoon until it becomes soft dough. Possibly save 1 tbsp. spelt flakes for rolling out the dough, as this might make it more manageable.

Roll the dough into sausages and put them in the fridge to cool. Once the dough is cold, slice the sausages into cookies of approx. ½ cm in width before placing them on a baking sheet covered with baking paper.

Bake the cookies for 10-12 minutes at 170° C, until they are crisp and golden. Take the cookies from the oven and leave them to cool.

Serve the cookies with a good cup of coffee or place them in an airtight container and save them for your next fishing trip.

Tip: You can use oat flakes instead of spelt flakes and you can substitute blueberries with other dried berries and fruit.

Fried plaice with cauliflower and crown dill 37 · Baked plaice with carrots, shallots and basil 41 · Steamed plaice with soft herb butter, beans and hazelnuts 44 · Whole fried plaice with mushrooms, new onions and parsley 47

PLAICE

FRIED PLAICE

WITH CAULIFLOWER AND CROWN DILL

4 PEOPLE

1 cauliflower

1 crown dill (the flowering head of
   dill stem if allowed to grow.
   Otherwise ordinary dill is fine)

100 ml olive oil

sea salt and freshly ground pepper

4 large double plaice fillets

a little rye flour

10 g butter

a little olive oil

1 unwaxed lemon

Chop the cauliflower into large florets, but slice a couple of them finely, if necessary use a mandolin. Place the chopped pieces of cauliflower in a bowl with cold water. Fry the cauliflower florets and crown dill in a little olive oil for 2-3 minutes, until slightly brown and tender. Add a little salt and freshly ground pepper. Remove the cauliflower florets from the frying pan, place them in a bowl and keep warm.

Wipe the frying pan clean before adding a little oil and butter. Allow the butter to sizzle. Cover the plaice fillets in rye flour and add salt and pepper to taste. Fry the plaice fillets for approx. 1 minute on each side, until beautifully golden and crisp on the outside while remaining succulent in the middle.

Remove the fillets from the pan and serve them with the fried cauliflower, finely chopped raw cauliflower, crown dill, lemon zest and juice and a little of butter from the frying pan. Delicious with some good bread and a green salad.

Baked plaice with carrots, shallots and basil

BAKED PLAICE

WITH CARROTS, SHALLOTS AND BASIL

4 PEOPLE

4 whole plaice

salt and freshly ground pepper

4 shallots

8 carrots with green tops left on

1 unwaxed lemon

1 bunch basil

500 ml olive oil

Make sure the plaice are fresh. Skin the plaice and clean out blood and intestines before rinsing them thoroughly in cold water (do ask your fishmonger to do it for you if this sounds a little too much to undertake at home). Cut each plaice into 2–3 smaller pieces and place in an ovenproof dish. Sprinkle with a little salt and some freshly ground pepper.

Peel the shallots and slice them finely. Rinse the carrots and cut them into smaller pieces. Place carrots and shallots, slices of lemon and basil on top of the plaice and drizzle with olive oil before placing the dish in the oven.

Bake the plaice and vegetables at 170° C for 15–17 minutes, until the fish is done and the vegetables tender. Take the dish out of the oven and serve the fish right away with some good bread and boiled potatoes.

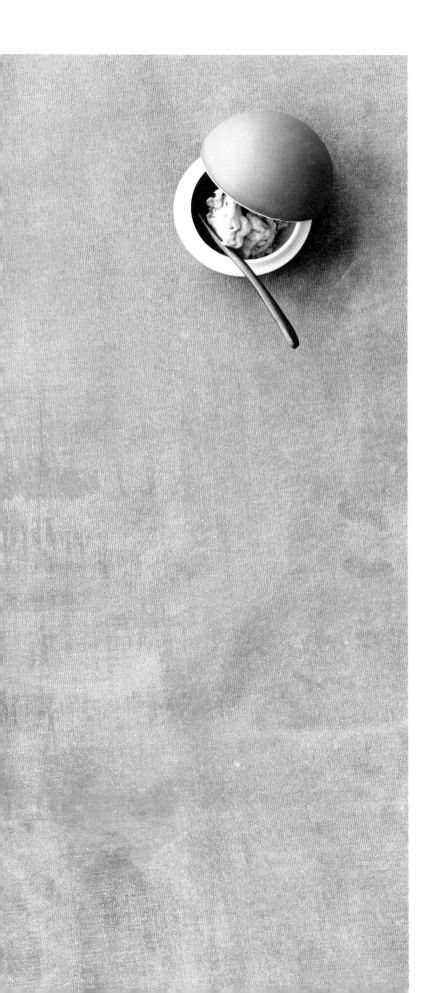

Steamed plaice with soft herb butter, beans and hazelnuts

POACHED PLAICE

WITH SOFT HERB BUTTER, GREEN BEANS AND HAZELNUTS

4 PEOPLE

200 g green beans

2 tbsp. olive oil

1 tbsp. cider vinegar

salt and freshly ground pepper

4 double fillets plaice

500 ml white wine

500 ml water

50 g fresh hazelnuts

or 25 g dried hazelnuts

½ bunch flat leaf parsley

Top and tail the beans before blanching them in salt water for 1–2 minutes. Refresh them in cold water right away. Strain the water from the beans and put them in a bowl to marinate in a little oil, vinegar, salt and freshly ground pepper.

Put the plaice fillets in a large pot and add white wine, water, salt and freshly ground pepper. Cover with a lid and bring it to the boil. Cook the plaice fillets for 1–2 minutes, then switch off the heat and leave the fish to marinate in the broth for about 5 minutes.

Take the plaice fillets from the pan and serve them in a deep dish or bowl with a knob of herb butter and marinated beans. Finally, sprinkle with chopped fresh hazelnuts and parsley.

Tip: What are double fillets of plaice? Each plaice has four fillets, 2 on top and 2 on the underside. You can fillet them individually (4 fillets) or you can avoid separating the 2 fillets on the same side, which gives you 2 double ones.

60 g butter

1 bunch flat leaved parsley

1 clove garlic

1 unwaxed lemon

1 tbsp. Soy sauce

salt and freshly ground pepper

HERB BUTTER

Place the butter in a bowl and mix in finely chopped parsley and garlic as well as lemon zest and juice, soy, salt and freshly ground pepper. Cream together until it becomes soft and smooth. Place a small dollop of herb butter on top of the poached plaice fillets or serve in a separate dish on the side.

FRIED WHOLE PLAICE

WITH MUSHROOMS, PEARL ONIONS AND PARSLEY

4 PEOPLE

4 whole plaice
wholegrain wheat flour
sea salt and freshly ground pepper
100 g butter
4 pearl onions with green shoots
10 g butter
200 chanterelles
2 tbsp. elderflower vinegar
1 bunch flat leaved parsley

Make sure the plaice are fresh. Rinse out blood and intestines before rinsing them thoroughly in cold water (or ask your fishmonger to do it for you). Cover the plaice in flour mixed with salt and pepper.

Melt the butter in a hot frying pan and wait for the sizzling foam to die down before frying the plaice for 3–4 minutes on each side, until they are nicely golden on both sides (more than likely, you'll only be able to fry one plaice at a time, unless you have a very big frying pan, so you might benefit from having two frying pans on the go simultaneously).

Chop off the top (but leave a little) and the bottom of the onions. Quarter them and place them in a covered saucepan with a little water, salt and 10 grams butter. Steam the onions underneath a lid for approx. 2 minutes until they become tender yet retain a little bite. Take the onions off the heat and leave them in the saucepan with a lid on until ready to serve

Clean the chanterelles and cut them into smaller pieces. Fry them in a little butter for 2–3 minutes. Add salt and pepper to taste before removing them from the frying pan.

Rinse the parsley and nip the leaves from the stalks. Serve the plaice with the steamed new onions, chanterelles and the butter from the frying pan to which you add a little vinegar. Garnish with chopped parsley.

Tip: A good way of making sure the plaice is actually done is by locating the pointy bone right beneath the place the head would be. If you can effortlessly pull out this bone, the plaice is done. If, on the other hand, it feels stuck, you need to fry the plaice a little longer.

Fried mackerel with sweetcorn, kohlrabi and bronze fennel 52 · Grilled mackerel with salted blackberries and candy beets 55 · Fried pickled mackerel with tomato, nectarine and pine 56 · Rye bread with new potatoes, smoked mackerel, smoked mayo, radishes and garden nasturtium 59 · Salted mackerel with pumpkin, kumquat, roasted buckwheat and wood sorrel 60 · Whole salt and herb baked mackerel with lemon and fennel 66

MACKEREL

FRIED MACKEREL

WITH SWEETCORN, KOHLRABI AND BRONZE FENNEL

4 PEOPLE

2 whole mackerels

2 corn on the cob

1 kohlrabi

2 tbsp. olive oil

25 g butter

1 unwaxed lemon

a little bronze fennel

salt and freshly ground pepper

Fillet the mackerels. Make sure you remove all bones, alternatively you can buy filleted mackerel from any fishmonger. Place the fillets on a plate and sprinkle with a little salt. Leave them for 10 minutes.

Slice the corn from the cobs and place them in a bowl. Peel the kohlrabi and chop it into cubes of 1 x 1 cm.

Heat a frying pan and fry the mackerel fillets in a little oil, skin side down, for approx. 2 minutes, until the skin is crisp and golden. Turn the fillets over and fry them for another 30 seconds. Then slide them back on the plate.

Add butter to the frying pan and fry the sweet corn and kohlrabi for 1-2 minutes. Add salt and pepper to taste before adding lemon zest and juice as well as chopped bronze fennel.

Place sweet corn and kohlrabi over the mackerel fillets and garnish with a little bronze fennel. Serve the fish right away with some good bread and a small salad.

GRILLED MACKEREL

WITH SALTED BLACKBERRIES AND CANDY CANE BEETS

4 PEOPLE

2 whole mackerels or 4 fillets

100 ml good olive oil

salt

10 thyme sprigs

4 fresh candy cane beets

200 ml salted blackberries

sea salt and freshly ground pepper

500 g fresh or frozen blackberries

10 g salt

Make sure the mackerels are fresh (ask your fishmonger to fillet them if necessary, although most will have already done that). Marinate the mackerel fillets in a little olive oil, salt and thyme and leave them for 10 minutes before cooking them on a grill pan.

Clean the candy cane beets and slice them finely on a mandolin before placing them in a bowl with cold water. Mix the salted blackberries with water and olive oil in a separate dish.

Grill the mackerel fillets on a hot grill pan, skin side down, for approx. 2 minutes, until the skin is crisp and golden. Turn the fillets over and grill them for another 30 seconds, until they're done but remain succulent in the middle.

Remove the fillets from the grill pan and serve them with thin slices of candy cane beet and blackberry dressing. Sprinkle a little thyme and sea salt on top.

SALTED BLACKBERRIES

Place blackberries and salt in a pickle jar and stir well. Leave the berries in the jar on the kitchen table without a lid for 4–5 days, until they start fermenting. Remember to stir the berries a little each day, but do nothing more.

After 5 days, put a lid on the jar and put the blackberries in the fridge or somewhere cool. The blackberries are now ready for use.

FRIED PICKLED MACKEREL

WITH TOMATO, NECTARINE AND EDIBLE PINE SHOOTS

4–6 PEOPLE

4 whole mackerels or 8 fillets
   (300–400 g each)
2 tbsp. salt
freshly ground pepper
1 red onion
2 nectarines
20 small tomatoes
300 ml water
300 ml cider vinegar, white wine vinegar
   or any other light, fruity vinegar
15 fresh pine-shoots
10 whole black peppercorns
100 g sugar

Day 1 – Make sure the mackerel are fresh. Clean, rinse and fillet the mackerels (or ask your fishmonger to do it for you).

Fry the fillets in a little oil on a hot frying pan, skin side down, for approx. 2 minutes, until the skin is crisp and golden, leaving the meaty side a little raw. Add salt and pepper to taste before removing the fillets from the pan and placing them in a dish, flesh side down.

Peel the onion and slice it finely. Peel the nectarines and slice them. Place onion, nectarines and tomatoes in a saucepan with water, vinegar, pine-shoots, whole peppercorns and sugar and bring to the boil. Pour this marinade over the mackerel fillets as soon as it boils, and leave the fillets to marinate in the warm pickle. Leave, covered, in the fridge until the following day.

Day 2 – Take the mackerel fillets from the fridge and serve them as they are with pickled vegetables on a slice of rye bread and garnish with a little finely chopped fennel. You can serve these mackerel fillets for lunch as well as dinner. For dinner you can serve them with boiled new potatoes or baked root vegetables. You can also heat the fillets in the dish at 160° C for 8-10 minutes.

Tip: Pine shoots are an acknowledged and increasingly available wild edible. Spruce pine is particularly tasty. The key to cooking with the tips of evergreen trees is to harvest them in spring, when they first begin to emerge from their brown papery casings. At this stage, spruce tips are very tender and have a fresh flavor that tastes lightly of resin with hints of citrus.

OPEN SANDWICH ON RYE BREAD

WITH NEW POTATOES, SMOKED MACKEREL, SMOKED MAYONNAISE, RADISHES AND GARDEN NASTURTIUM

4 PEOPLE

1 smoked mackerel

500 g new potatoes

6 radishes

1 pot of garden nasturtium

salt and freshly ground pepper

4 slices hearty rye bread

300 ml rapeseed oil

4 egg yolks

1 tbsp. mustard

3 tbsp. cider vinegar

salt and freshly ground pepper

Skin and pluck the bones from the mackerel and place the meat on a plate before covering it with cling film. Place skin and bones in a saucepan, add the rapeseed oil and carefully heat until the oil reaches 50–60° C. Take the saucepan off the heat and leave the oil to cool and draw its flavour from the fish bones.

Rinse the potatoes and place them in a saucepan with water and a pinch of salt. Boil the potatoes, covered, for 8-10 minutes. Then turn the heat off and leave them to finish cooking.

MAYONNAISE

Whisk egg yolks, mustard, salt and freshly ground pepper until 'white' and creamy. Then whisk in the now cool and sieved mackerel-oil little by little, to make sure that the eggs absorb the oil. Keep whisking until there is no more oil left and the mayonnaise is creamy and thick. Add a little salt and freshly ground pepper to taste if needed.

Spread mayonnaise on four slices of rye bread and place the still warm, boiled halved potatoes on the bread slices before adding bits of smoked mackerel, thinly sliced radishes and garden nasturtiums on top. Add a little salt and freshly ground pepper to taste and serve for lunch.

SALTED MACKEREL

WITH PUMPKIN, KUMQUAT, FRIED BUCKWHEAT AND WOOD SORREL

4 PEOPLE

1 mackerel

1 tsp. sea salt

1 pumpkin (butternut squash)

100 ml olive oil

4 kumquats

2 tbsp. cider vinegar

1 tsp. liquid honey

salt & freshly ground pepper

2 tbsp. buckwheat

2 handful redwood sorrel

Make sure the mackerel is fresh. It's very important that it's completely fresh, as in this recipe it'll only be 'salted' and not cooked. Fillet the mackerel (unless your fishmonger does it for you) and make sure to remove all bones. Place the mackerel fillets on a plate or a dish, skin-side down, and sprinkle with salt. Cover the fillets in cling film and leave them in the fridge for 6-12 hours.

Peel the pumpkin and slice finely. Cover the pumpkin slices in a little olive oil before grilling them on a hot grill pan for approx. 2 minutes each side, until tender and nicely charred.

Finely slice the kumquats and place the slices in a bowl with vinegar, honey, the remaining oil, salt and freshly ground pepper and mix into a dressing. Take the pumpkin slices off the pan and toss with the dressing while warm, as this will help them absorb the dressing and the kumquat taste.

Fry the buckwheat on a dry frying pan until the grains turn golden and start 'popping'.

Slice the mackerel fillets finely and place them on a plate with slices of pumpkin covered in kumquat dressing and sprinkle fried buckwheat and wood sorrel on top. Add salt and freshly ground pepper to taste.

Tip: *Oxalis oregana* (redwood sorrel, Oregon oxalis) is an edible wild plant that has been consumed by humans around the world for a millennia. Used for all sorts of medicinal purposes by the Native American tribes in the USA, it is now widely grown all over Europe. The redwood variety used here is particularly noted for its fresh, lemony flavour.

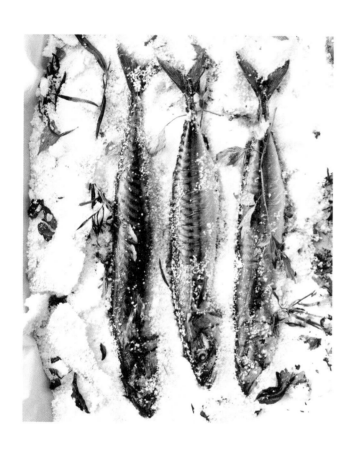

Salt and herb baked whole mackerel with lemon and fennel

SALT AND HERB BAKED WHOLE MACKEREL

WITH LEMON AND FENNEL

2–3 whole mackerels, depending
on size
2 handful mixed herbs
    (mint, tarragon, lovage, thyme
    and parsley)
1 lemon
approx. 2 kg coarse salt

Clean and gut the mackerels and rinse them thoroughly in cold water (or place your faith in the fishmonger once more). Then wipe them dry with kitchen towel.

Pour salt into a large ovenproof dish and place the mackerels on top. Then cover with fresh herbs, slices of lemon and the remaining salt, almost covering the fish completely.

Bake the mackerels in the oven for 20–25 minutes at 170° C, until the salt hardens to a crust around the fish. Make sure the fish is cooked but remains succulent in the middle.

Take the fish from the oven and leave them to settle for 5 minutes, before removing the salt crust. Then gently remove the fish meat off the bones and serve with a crisp fennel salad.

You can use this recipe with other whole fish as well, including redfish, gurnard, weever, zander or perch. It is, however, important that you use whole fish and not fillets, as the salt will penetrate the fillets to a degree that would be unpalatable.

2 fennel bulbs

2 shallots

1 bunch tarragon

salt and freshly ground pepper

3 tbsp. olive oil

1 lemon

FENNEL SALAD

Top and tail the fennels before slicing them finely. You can use
a mandolin or a very sharp knife. Then place the fennel slices in a
bowl with cold water.

Peel the shallots and slice them finely. Rinse the tarragon and chop
coarsely. Drain water from the fennel slices and let them drip dry.
Then toss fennel with shallots and tarragon before marinating with
salt, freshly ground pepper and olive oil.

Halve the lemon. Heat a dry frying pan and place the lemon
halves on the pan, cut side down. Fry the lemon halves for
4–5 minutes, until they're well charred.

Serve the charred lemon halves with the salt-baked mackerel and
fennel salad. Squeeze lemon juice on the fish before eating.

Hot-smoked garfish with pickled green tomatoes 74 · Deep fried garfish with cauliflower, sea buckthorn and tarragon 76 · Fried garfish with cucumber, radish and parsley 79 · Grilled whole garfish à la latino with lime, pickled red onions, coriander, mint and yoghurt 82 · Fried garfish with Jerusalem artichoke, apple, elderberry and wood sorrel 85

GARFISH

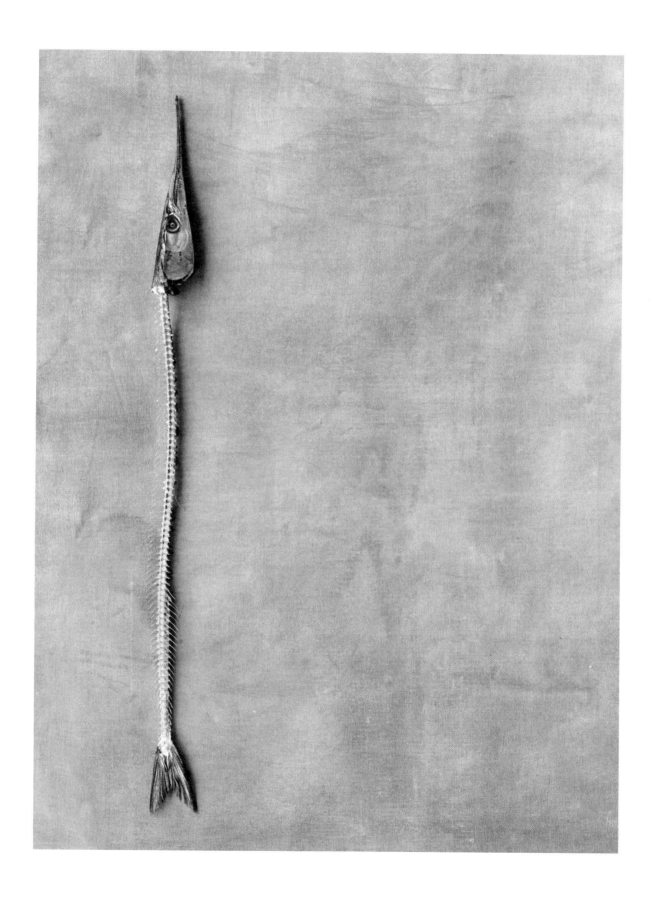

Hot smoked garfish with pickled green tomatoes

HOT-SMOKED GARFISH

WITH PICKLED GREEN TOMATOES

4 PEOPLE

2 whole garfish
salt
2 handful smoke-dust
a short piece of string

Clean the garfish thoroughly and rinse well in cold water to make sure that there's no blood or intestines left. Wipe them dry and place them in a dish. Sprinkle with salt and leave them for 1 hour.

Tie fish tails and beaks together, to make garfish rings. This is to ensure that the fish is more evenly smoked than if merely hanging straight down, as one end would be close to the smoke and the other end far removed from the smoke. This way, the fish will take up less space in the smoke oven as well.

Hang the fish inside the oven and place the smoke-dust in an old two handled saucepan before heating it on the stove until it starts to smoke. Then place the saucepan in the oven and close the oven door. Turn the heat to 60-70° C and smoke the garfish for 15-20 minutes, until their skin is nicely golden and the meat just cooked. You can also smoke garfish in a barbecue or home smoking chamber (if you have one).

Take the garfish out of the oven and let them rest for 15-20 minutes before removing the skin and flaking the meat off the bones. Serve the smoked garfish with pickled green tomatoes and possibly toast and a hearty salad.

Tip: What is smoke-dust? Smoke dust is the result of finely ground sustainable woods, dried to below 16%. Easily available from all specialist and garden stores, on and offline, you can choose from oak, beech, hickory, whiskey oak, apple and cherry woods.

1 kg green tomatoes

1 litre cider vinegar

1 litre water

500 g sugar

1 cinnamon stick

2 star anises

1 dried red chilli

10 whole black pepper corns

2 shallots

1 tbsp. salt

PICKLED GREEN TOMATOES

Rinse the tomatoes in cold water before quartering the bigger ones and pricking a hole in the smaller ones. Bring vinegar, water, sugar and spices to the boil before adding the tomatoes to the boiling liquid. Leave them in there for 2 minutes and then take the pot off the heat and let the tomatoes cool in the pickle.

Peel the shallots and add them to the tomatoes and brine before pouring all of it into a pickle jar. Leave the tomatoes to mature for at least 4–5 days, preferably a couple of weeks, before serving.

Serve the pickled tomatoes with smoked garfish.

DEEP FRIED GARFISH

WITH CAULIFLOWER, SEA BUCKTHORN AND TARRAGON

4 PEOPLE

100 ml sea buckthorn (fresh or frozen)

50 ml sugar

50 ml water

1 tbsp. cider vinegar

50 ml olive oil

1 garfish fillet

100 ml wheat flour

½ cauliflower

2 litres rapeseed oil

sea salt and freshly ground pepper

1 bunch tarragon

Place sea buckthorn, sugar, water and vinegar in a saucepan and bring to the boil, then simmer for 5–7 minutes over a low heat, until it turns into a thick compote. Take the pan off the heat and stir in olive oil, while the sea buckthorns are still warm, until the mixture resembles a smooth dressing. Leave it to cool.

Make sure there are no bones left in the skinless garfish fillet before slicing it finely and tossing the strips in flour.

Slice the cauliflower very finely with a mandolin or a very sharp knife and place the cauliflower in a bowl with cold water, to keep it fresh. Then drain the cauliflower through a sieve.

Heat the 2 litres of rapeseed oil in a deep saucepan – use a match to test if the oil's hot enough for frying (it'll start sizzling around the match when lowered into the oil). Make sure, though, that the oil doesn't get too warm as it will burn. Place the garfish strips in the hot oil, a few at a time, and fry until golden and crispy. Take the crispy fish strips out of the oil and let them drain on a piece of kitchen towel. Sprinkle with sea salt.

Serve the crispy garfish fritters with finely sliced cauliflower, sea buckthorn dressing and tarragon as a starter or as part of a tasting menu.

FRIED GARFISH

WITH CUCUMBER, RADISH AND PARSLEY

4 PEOPLE

2 garfish fillets

2 tbsp. mustard

salt and freshly ground pepper

a little flour

8 radishes

1 cucumber

3 tbsp. cider vinegar

1 tbsp. liquid honey

1 bunch parsley

100 ml olive oil

2 tbsp. rapeseed oil

10 g butter

Make sure the fillets are boneless and slice them into 8 pieces. Spread mustard on the inside of the fillets and sprinkle with salt and freshly ground pepper before folding them and tossing them in flour.

Top and tail the radishes before slicing them finely with a mandolin. Place them in a bowl. Then slice the cucumber finely and place the slices in the bowl with the radishes. Add vinegar, honey, salt and freshly ground pepper to the bowl and toss well before leaving radishes and cucumber to marinate for 5 minutes, until soft but still crisp.

Rinse and strip the parsley leaves from their stems. Place parsley leaves and olive oil in a blender (save a little parsley for garnish) and blend until it becomes green oil. Pour the oil through a finely meshed sieve, which gives you very green and pure oil.

Heat a frying pan and add rapeseed oil and butter. Then place the garfish pieces on the pan and fry them for 2 minutes on each side, until they become golden and crisp on the outside.

Take the pieces of fish off the pan and place them on a plate and garnish with slices of marinated cucumber and radish. Then sprinkle a little marinade and parsley oil on top before finishing garnishing with chopped parsley and sea salt. Serve the fish straight away with boiled potatoes or good bread.

Whole grilled garfish à la latino with lime, pickled red onion, coriander, mint and yoghurt

WHOLE GRILLED GARFISH À LA LATINO

WITH LIME, PICKLED RED ONION, CORIANDER, MINT AND YOGHURT

4 PEOPLE

———

2 whole garfish

1 tbsp. fennel seeds

1 tbsp. coriander seeds

1 tbsp. cumin

1 tsp. dried chilli

2 tbsp. olive oil

2 red onions

2 limes

1 tsp. liquid honey

1 bunch coriander

1 bunch mint

200 ml yoghurt

salt and freshly ground pepper

Clean the garfish thoroughly and rinse in cold water, to make sure that there's no blood or intestines left (remember your fishmonger...) Cut the heads and fins off and then cut the garfish into pieces of approx. 10 cm lengthwise. Sprinkle with a little salt.

Crush the spices lightly in a pestle and mortar, and place them on a flat dish. Roll the garfish in the spices so that the fish can absorb their flavours as much as possible.

Peel the red onions and slice them finely. Place them in a bowl with lime zest and juice, honey, salt and freshly ground pepper. Leave the onions to marinate and soften. This will rid them of their tanginess while remaining crunchy.

Grill the garfish on a very hot barbecue or grill pan for 2-3 minutes on each side, which will give them a beautifully golden and crispy skin, and the spices will be well charred, allowing the fish meat to absorb the taste.

Take the garfish off the barbecue or grill pan and serve immediately with pickled red onions, yoghurt, coriander and mint. Serve as a lunch dish or as a light main dish with some good bread.

FRIED GARFISH

WITH JERUSALEM ARTICHOKE, APPLE, ELDERBERRY AND WOOD SORREL

4 PEOPLE

2 garfish fillets

a little flour

4 Jerusalem artichokes

100 ml elderberries (fresh or frozen)

50 ml cider vinegar

2 tbsp. sugar

50 ml olive oil

2 tbsp. rapeseed oil

salt and freshly ground pepper

2 apples

½ pot wood sorrel

Make sure you remove all bones and fins from the garfish (cut them off if necessary). Sprinkle the garfish fillets with salt and pepper and cut them into 8 pieces. Fold them with their skin side out and toss them in a little flour. Then leave the fish to settle for 5–10 minutes.

Rinse the Jerusalem artichokes thoroughly and leave their skin on. Place the elderberries in a saucepan with vinegar, sugar and olive oil. Bring to the boil and let the liquid simmer for 1–2 minutes before removing the pot from the heat. Let the elderberries marinate for another 5–10 minutes.

Heat a frying pan with rapeseed oil. Place the garfish pieces on the pan and fry for approx. 2 minutes on each side, which will give them a beautifully golden crust on both sides. Sprinkle with salt and freshly ground pepper to taste.

Finely slice the Jerusalem artichokes and apples with a mandolin or a sharp knife.

Place the garfish fillets on a plate and add the finely sliced Jerusalem artichokes and apples before pouring the warm elderberry vinaigrette on top. Finally, garnish with a little wood sorrel and serve the fish as a lunch dish or a main dish with boiled potatoes and bread.

Fried langoustine with pumpkin purée, chanterelles and almonds 89 · Langoustine soup with courgette, fennel and mint 94 ·
Barbecued langoustine with carrot, raspberry, crisp rye bread and sea sandwort 96 · Langoustine tempura with fennel, wood sorrel
and charred lemon 99 · Elderflower-barbecued langoustine tails with smoked mayonnaise and bitter lettuce 102

LANGOUSTINE

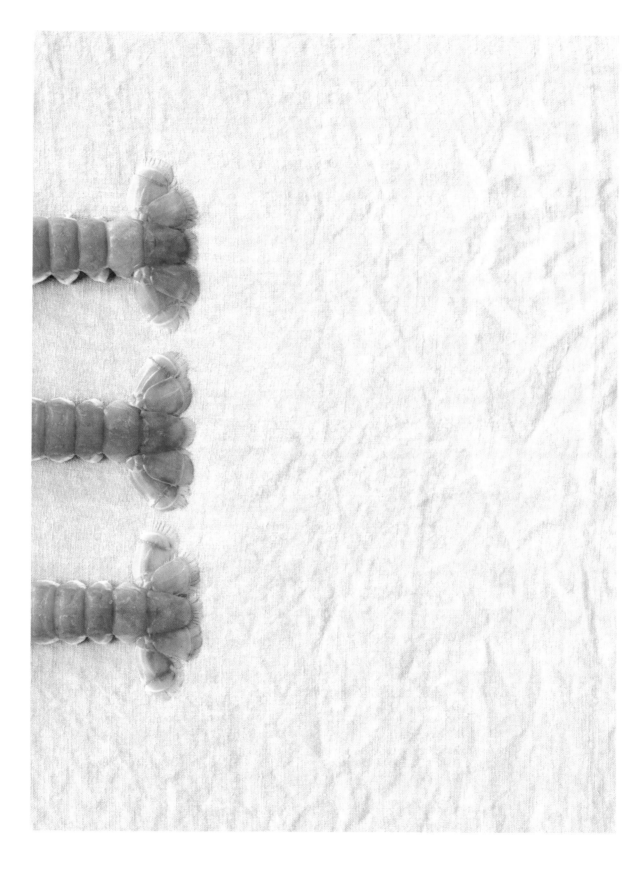

FRIED LANGOUSTINE

WITH PUMPKIN PURÉE, CHANTERELLES AND ALMONDS

4 PEOPLE

8–12 langoustines

300 g chanterelles

salt and freshly ground pepper

25 g almonds

50 ml olive oil

a little bronze fennel

1 Hokkaido pumpkin

25 g butter

50 ml cider vinegar

sea salt and freshly ground pepper

1 tbsp. liquid honey

Shell the langoustines and place the tails on a dish. Sprinkle with a little salt and leave them to absorb the flavours for 5–10 minutes (freeze the heads and shells for a soup or broth as they're extremely flavoursome – in fact, just see the next recipe on p94).

Clean the chanterelles with a brush or a paring knife. If they're very dirty, you can rinse them in a little cold water. Then fry them on a hot pan in a little oil for 2–3 minutes, which will give them a little colour and tenderise them. Add salt and freshly ground pepper to taste.

Remove the chanterelles from the pan and then fry the langoustine tails, using the oil that is left in the frying pan, as this will add flavour to the langoustine tails. Fry the langoustines for approx. 1 minute on each side, until nicely fried on the outside yet still succulent in the middle. Add salt and freshly ground pepper to taste.

Serve the fried langoustine with pumpkin purée, chanterelles, chopped almonds and chopped bronze fennel. Drizzle a little olive oil on top.

PUMPKIN PURÉE

Split the pumpkin and remove the seeds with a spoon before chopping the pumpkin flesh into big chunks. Place the chunks in a saucepan and cover with water. Bring to the boil and boil the pumpkin for approx. 20 minutes, until tender, and then drain.

Place the boiled pumpkin chunks in a blender and add butter, vinegar, salt, pepper and honey before blending until the purée is smooth. Pour the purée back into the saucepan and heat it. Add extra vinegar, salt and pepper if necessary.

Langoustine soup with courgette, fennel and mint

LANGOUSTINE SOUP

WITH COURGETTE, FENNEL AND MINT

4 PEOPLE

2 onions

2 cloves garlic

4–5 tomatoes

½ fennel

1 kg langoustine shells
and heads

1 tbsp. olive oil

10 thyme sprigs

10 whole black pepper corns

200 ml white wine

approx. 2 litres water

100 ml cream

cider vinegar

sugar

sea salt

Prep the herbs – onion, garlic, tomatoes and fennel – by chopping them coarsely.

Heat a large deep frying pan and fry the langoustine shells and heads in some olive oil for 3-4 minutes, without charring them (it's important that the shells are thoroughly browned as this will bring out the taste in the stock).

Then add all herbs and sauté for another minute. Then add white wine and reduce the liquid to half before adding water to cover the shells. Bring the stock to the boil and skim the froth to get rid of impurities. Turn the heat down and let the stock simmer for 20 minutes. Remove the pan from the heat and leave it to infuse for another 20 minutes.

Sieve the stock through a finely meshed sieve and use a spoon to mash the shells and herbs to ensure that you get every ounce of taste from them before discarding them. Pour the stock back into a pot and reduce the liquid to half, as this will intensify the taste. Add a little cream and bring the stock to the boil for 4–5 minutes. Finally add a little vinegar, sugar and salt to taste.

4 langoustines

salt and freshly ground pepper

1 green courgette

2 tbsp. olive oil

1 unwaxed lemon

½ bunch mint

GARNISH

Shell the langoustines (use their shells in the bisque), and place the tails on a plate and sprinkle with a little salt. Leave them to absorb the flavour for 10 minutes.

Rinse the courgette and chop finely. Heat a frying pan with a little olive oil and fry the langoustine tails for approx. 30 seconds on either side, to make sure that they're nicely fried on the outside and still succulent in the middle.

Remove the langoustine tails from the pan and fry the courgettes at great heat for 30 seconds, adding colour while retaining their crispiness. Remove the pan from the heat and add salt, freshly ground pepper, lemon zest and juice and a little chopped mint.

Serve the courgette mixture in bowls or deep dishes and place the langoustine tails on top before pouring the bisque. Garnish with a little mint and serve the soup immediately.

GRILLED LANGOUSTINE

WITH CARROT, RASPBERRY, CRISPY RYE BREAD AND SEA SANDWORT

4 PEOPLE

12 langoustines

4 garden carrots

100 g fresh raspberries

50 ml cider vinegar

1 tbsp. liquid honey

50 ml olive oil

salt and freshly ground pepper

1 handful sea sandwort

8-12 very thin slice of rye bread
   (1–2 mm)

2 tbsp. olive oil

sea salt

Peel the langoustine and place the tails on a plate. Sprinkle with a little salt.

Rinse the carrots and slice them lengthways into thin strips. Use a mandolin. Place the strips in a bowl with cold water, so they remain crisp.

Put raspberries in a bowl and gently mash them with a fork. Add vinegar, honey, oil (save a little for frying), salt and freshly ground pepper and mix into a thick vinaigrette.

Heat a frying pan and fry the langoustine tails in a little olive oil for approx. 30 seconds each side, to make sure they're wonderfully golden on the outside while remaining succulent in the middle. Add salt and freshly ground pepper to taste.

Remove the tails from the pan and serve with the crispy carrot strips, raspberry vinaigrette, sea sandwort and crispy rye bread on top. Serve as a lunch dish or as part of a tasting menu.

CRISPY RYE BREAD

Place the slices of rye bread on a baking sheet with baking paper and drizzle with olive oil before sprinkling sea salt on top. Bake the rye bread in the oven for approx. 10 minutes at 170° C, until crispy and golden. Remove the slices of rye bread from the oven and leave them to cool before using them as garnish for the langoustine.

Tip: What is sea sandwort? You can find this succulent green plant growing anywhere along the seashores of Europe and North America. As soon as you see it you'll be amazed you never knew it was edible.

LANGOUSTINE TEMPURA

WITH FENNEL, WOOD SORREL AND CHARRED LEMON

4 PEOPLE

8 langoustines

sea salt and freshly ground pepper

1 fennel

1 lemon

2 tbsp. olive oil

2 litre rapeseed oil

½ portion of tempura batter (cold)

a little wood sorrel

Shell the langoustine and place the tails on a plate before sprinkling them with a little salt.

Finely slice the fennel on a mandolin and place the fennel slices in a bowl with cold water. Halve the lemon and heat a dry frying pan. Place the lemon halves on the pan, cut side down, and fry the lemon for 4–5 minutes, until well charred.

Pour the rapeseed oil into a deep saucepan and heat it slowly until it reaches 150–160° C (check by sticking a match into the oil, if it sizzles around the match, the oil is ready for frying). Dip the langoustine tails in batter. Please note that the batter should be very cold. Then place the tails in the hot oil and fry four tails at a time, to make sure the oil does not lose heat. Remove the tails from the pot and let them drip off on kitchen towel. Sprinkle with sea salt. Fry the remaining four tails.

Serve the langoustine tails with the finely sliced fennel, drained and then tossed in olive oil. Sprinkle wood sorrel on top and serve immediately. Drizzle juice from the charred lemon halves on top. Serve this dish as a snack or a starter.

ELDERFLOWER-GRILLED LANGOUSTINE TAILS

WITH SMOKED MAYONNAISE AND BITTER LETTUCE

4 PEOPLE

16 langoustine tails

4–5 elderflowers

   (you can also use other edible

   flowers or herbs)

3 tbsp. olive oil

sea salt

1 head radicchio

½ head curly endive

2 pasteurised egg yolks

1 tbsp. mustard

1 tbsp. cider vinegar

1 tbsp. smoked salt

freshly ground pepper

150 ml rape- or grape seed oil

Place the langoustine tails in an ovenproof dish or a roasting tray and place the elderflowers on top. Drizzle with olive oil before sprinkling with sea salt.

Divide the heads of lettuce into smaller chunks. Then rinse and allow them to drip dry.

Place the langoustine tails in a pre-heated oven at 230° C (possibly under the grill) and bake/grill them for approx. 5 minutes, until cooked. The smell is wonderful. Remove them from the oven and let them rest for 1–2 minutes before serving them with smoked mayonnaise and lettuce.

SMOKED MAYONNAISE

Whisk egg yolks, mustard, vinegar, smoked salt and white pepper in a food mixer or with an electric mixer. Then slowly add the oil while whisking rigorously to keep the mayo from separating. When you've added the oil you can add extra vinegar, salt and pepper to taste.

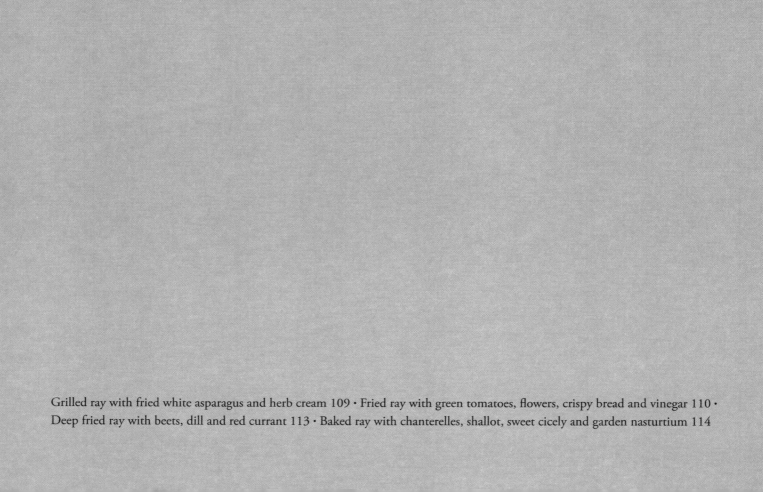

RAY

GRILLED RAY

WITH FRIED WHITE ASPARAGUS AND HERB CREAM

4 PEOPLE

8 white asparagus

salt and freshly ground pepper

600 g ray wing fillet

50 ml olive oil

15 g butter

1 head curly endive

200 ml natural yoghurt

1 tsp. Dijon mustard

1 tsp. liquid honey

1 unwaxed lemon

salt and freshly ground pepper

½ bunch dill

½ bunch tarragon

Peel the white asparagus and break off the tougher ends of the stems. Heat a frying pan and add a little oil and butter and fry the white asparagus for approx. 1 minute all over, to ensure an evenly golden surface. They should be tender but not without a little bite in the middle. Remove the asparagus from the pan and sprinkle with salt and freshly ground pepper.

Divide the ray fillet into four pieces and drizzle with a little olive oil. Grill the pieces on a hot grill pan for 1–2 minutes on each side, to make sure they're nicely charred but remain succulent in the middle.

Tear the curly endive into smaller pieces and rinse thoroughly. Remove the ray fillets from the grill pan and sprinkle with salt and freshly ground pepper to taste. Cut the asparagus into 3–4 pieces each and serve them on a plate alongside the curly endive and the grilled ray fillet. Garnish with a little curly endive and some herbs. Serve as a starter or a main course with good bread and possibly a salad.

HERB CREAM

Pour the yoghurt into a bowl and mix in mustard, honey lemon zest and juice as well as salt and pepper. Chop dill and tarragon (save a little as final garnish) and add to the cream. Mix everything until it forms a smooth dressing.

FRIED RAY WINGS

WITH CAPERS, GREEN TOMATOES, FLOWERS, CRISP BREAD AND VINEGAR

4 PEOPLE

4 green tomatoes

2 tbsp. cider vinegar

salt and freshly ground pepper

600 g ray wing (same weight as fillet)

2 tbsp. olive oil (for frying)

50 g butter

2 tbsp. capers

1 handful thyme flowers
or any other herbal flowers

¼ loaf of day-old bread

2 tbsp. olive oil

sea salt

Rinse the tomatoes in cold water and dry thoroughly. Slice finely, preferably using a mandolin or a very sharp knife. Place the tomato slices in a bowl and carefully toss with vinegar, olive oil, salt and freshly ground pepper and then leave them to marinate for 5–10 minutes.

Divide the ray wings into four pieces. Heat a frying pan with oil and fry the ray pieces for 2 minutes on one side, to give them a nicely golden surface. Then turn the wings over and fry them for another 30 seconds.

Add butter to the pan and allow it to sizzle around the edges of the ray wings. Add salt and freshly ground pepper to taste. Make sure the frying pan is not too hot, as this will burn the butter, and you need the browned butter for the sauce. Add capers and caper vinegar and stir well before adding salt, freshly ground pepper and thyme to taste.

Serve the pieces of fried ray wing with melted butter, capers and thyme. Garnish with green tomatoes and crisp bread and serve immediately.

CRISPY BREAD
Finely slice the bread and place the slices on a baking sheet covered with baking paper and drizzle with olive oil before sprinkling sea salt on top.

Place the baking sheet in the oven and bake for 8–10 minutes at 180° C, until golden and crispy. Remove the bread slices from the oven and leave to cool. Use the crispy bread as garnish with the fried ray wing.

DEEP FRIED RAY WING FILLET

WITH BEETS, DILL AND REDCURRANTS

4 PEOPLE

400 g ray wing fillet

salt and freshly ground pepper

a little wheat flour

4 fresh beetroots with their tops

100 g fresh redcurrants

2 tbsp. cider vinegar

1 tsp. liquid honey

100 ml olive oil

2 litres rapeseed or corn oil

1 bunch dill

Make sure that there are no bones in the ray wings and that their membrane is fresh. Cut the wings into thin strips and sprinkle them with a little salt and pepper before tossing in flour.

Top and tail the beetroots and save the nicest looking leaves. Slice the beetroots finely on a mandolin and place them in a bowl with cold water to keep them crisp.

Hull the redcurrants from the stalks and put them in a bowl. Add vinegar, honey, oil, salt and pepper. Mix well. You can even mash some of the currants a little to release their juice before leaving the vinaigrette to marinate for a while.

Pour the 2 litres of oil into a large deep saucepan and heat it carefully. When the oil is hot enough, toss the strips of ray wing in flour and deep-fry them for 1-2 minutes, giving them a nicely golden surface while remaining succulent in the middle.

Sprinkle some sea salt on top of the ray wings and serve with finely sliced beetroots, beetroot top leaves, chopped dill and then finally drizzle the red currant vinaigrette on top. Serve the dish immediately while the fish is hot and crisp.

BAKED RAY WING FILLETS

WITH CHANTERELLE, SHALLOT, SWEET CICELY AND GARDEN NASTURTIUM

4 PEOPLE

600 g ray wing fillets

salt and freshly ground pepper

300 g chanterelles (cleaned weight)

2 shallots

1 clove garlic

2 tbsp. olive oil

15 g butter

½ unwaxed lemon

1 bunch sweet cicely

½ pot garden nasturtium

Divide the ray wing fillets into four pieces and place them in an ovenproof dish. Then drizzle with a little olive oil before sprinkling with salt and freshly ground pepper.

Clean the chanterelles with a brush or a small paring knife. If they're very dirty, you can rinse them in cold water. Cut the chanterelles into smaller pieces and let them dry off on a tea towel.

Peel the shallots and garlic clove and chop finely. Heat a frying pan and add 1 tbsp. olive oil and butter and fry the chanterelles for 2–3 minutes, until they're tender and gain a bit of colour. Then add finely chopped shallots and garlic alongside lemon zest and juice, sweet cicely as well as salt and freshly ground pepper to taste.

Place the ray wing fillets in the oven and bake for 8-10 minutes at 160° C, until the meat 'settles' but remains succulent in the middle.

Remove the fish from the oven and serve the fillets in deep dishes or bowls with the sautéed chanterelles on top. Then garnish with sweet cicely and garden nasturtium and serve as a lunch dish, a starter or as part of a tasting menu.

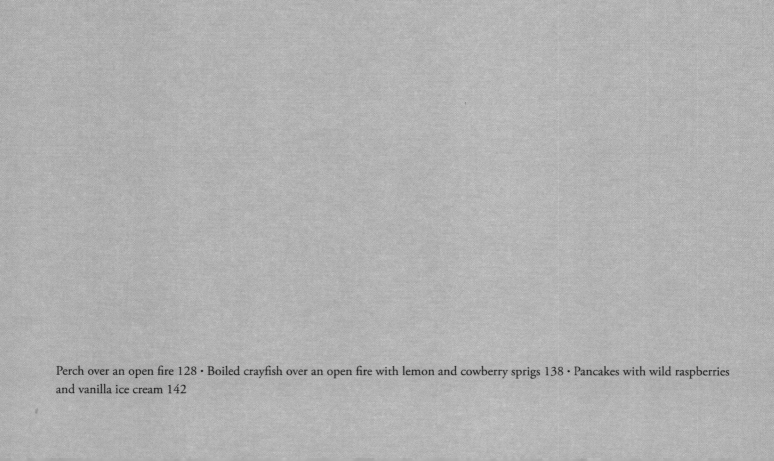

FROM THE LAKE

PERCH COOKED ON
AN OPEN FIRE

4 PEOPLE

4 perch, 350-400 g

salt and freshly ground pepper

heather

fern leaves

pine branches

1 long stick

steel wire or wet raffia rope

Clean the perch and rinse them thoroughly in cold water, to make sure that there are no blood or intestines left (there won't be a fishmonger available at this point!). Then sprinkle with salt and freshly ground pepper.

Dip the heather, fern leaves and pine in the lake or a bucket full of water and then wrap the perch in first heather, then fern leaves and finally pine branches. Wrap the 'packages' tightly with steel wire or wet raffia rope. It's important that the raffia rope is wet, as it may very quickly burn otherwise.

Now tie the 'package' horizontally to a stick, with the wire or raffia rope and place it horizontally over the fire. Having two y-shaped sticks at either end of the fire on which you can place the horizontal stick will prove advantageous (see my picture of how this is done on previous p124).

Now bake the perches over the open fire for approx. 20-30 minutes, depending on how hot the fire is. Remember to turn the stick to make sure that the perches are baked on all sides. Remove the perch-packages from the stick and unwrap them.

1 kg new potatoes

1 handful wild herbs, e.g. cowberry,
    nettles, dandelion leaves, wild garlic
    or whatever else you can find

a little salt

BOILED POTATOES WITH WILD HERBS

(Bring the ready cooked potatoes from your kitchen, if you feel the fire may not be hot enough to boil them outside).

Rinse the potatoes well. Put them in a saucepan and cover them with water. Add herbs and salt and bring the saucepan to the boil and boil the potatoes for 10 minutes over low heat. Then turn off the heat and leave the potatoes to finish cooking in the pan for another 5–7 minutes. Drain the potatoes and serve with creamed butter.

CREAMED BUTTER WITH HEATHER AND THYME FLOWERS

(If the butter is already soft enough, this can be made outside, but if not, stay in the kitchen and bring along with you)

Place the butter in a bowl and whisk in lemon zest and juice, salt and freshly ground pepper until it's really creamy. Serve the butter in a dish or bowl and garnish with heather and thyme. Serve with boiled potatoes.

200 g soft butter

½ unwaxed lemon

salt and freshly ground pepper

5 heather sprigs

5 thyme sprigs with flowers

BOILED CRAYFISH OVER AN OPEN FIRE

WITH LEMON AND COWBERRY SPRIGS

4 PEOPLE

1 kg live crayfish (about 20-25 crayfish)

1 unwaxed lemon

a few cowberry sprigs
  (you can also use dill, parsley
  or chervil)

salt

2 pasteurised egg yolks

1 tbsp. mustard

1 tbsp. cider vinegar

1 tsp. salt

freshly ground pepper

150 ml rape- or grape seed oil

40 g North Sea cheese
  (use Gouda or Comte as substitutes)

Add water, a couple of lemon slices, cowberry (or other herb) sprigs and salt to a deep saucepan and bring it to the boil over an open fire.

Add the crayfish when the water is boiling. The water will stop boiling once you add the crayfish, but leave them in there until the water starts to boil again, then remove the pot from the heat.

Take out the crayfish and serve them immediately while still warm. You can also leave them to cool in the water and eat them cold. Serve the crayfish with the fried mushroom flatbread and North Sea mayonnaise.

NORTH SEA MAYONNAISE

Whisk egg yolks, mustard, vinegar, salt and white pepper in a food mixer or with an electric mixer. Then slowly add oil while whisking vigorously to make sure the mayonnaise doesn't separate. Once you've added the oil add a little salt, pepper and possibly vinegar to taste. Finally, add freshly grated North Sea (or Gouda or Comte) cheese.

Serve the mayonnaise with the boiled crayfish. You can also use it to spread on a regular sandwich or as garnish on top of an open sandwich with egg or potato.

20 g dried mushrooms

10 g yeast

200 ml lukewarm water

100 ml dark beer

300 g wheat flour

8 g sea salt

100 g wholegrain spelt flour
   or wholegrain Öland-wheat

100 ml olive oil for frying

sea salt

MUSHROOOM FLATBREAD

Crush the dried mushrooms in a mortar or spice churn until powdery.

Dissolve yeast and mushroom-dust in water and beer and then add a little wheat flour before adding salt, as the salt may otherwise 'kill' some of the yeast cells. Then add the rest of the flour and knead until the dough is soft and smooth. Knead it well by lifting the dough with a wooden ladle until it comes away easily from the side of the bowl. Leave the dough to rise in the bowl for approx. 1 hour, until it's doubled in size.

Then pull the dough from the bowl with your hands and onto a flour-sprinkled kitchen top. Divide the dough into 8–10 lumps and pull or roll the lumps into thin flatbreads (much like pancakes). Fry them in some olive oil on a very hot pan for 1–2 minutes on each side, until crisp and golden. Then sprinkle with sea salt when they're all done and still warm.

Pancakes with wild raspberries and vanilla ice cream

PANCAKES

WITH WILD RASPBERRIES AND VANILLA ICECREAM

10–12 PANCAKES

100 ml wheat flour

1 pinch of salt

¼ vanilla pod

2 eggs

250 ml semi-skimmed milk

15 g butter

2 handfuls wild raspberries
(regular raspberries or other
berries would also be fine)

Whisk the flour, salt, vanilla grains, eggs and milk together. Melt the butter in a small saucepan and pour the hot butter into the batter while whisking until the batter is smooth and shiny. Let the batter rest for 1 hour in the fridge.

Cook the pancakes in a very hot frying pan – there's butter in the batter, but depending on the frying pan, you may need to add a little butter while cooking the pancakes.

Remove the pancakes from the frying pan and keep them warm in the oven. Spread a little sugar on top and cover with foil, to keep them from drying out. Serve with wild raspberries and vanilla ice cream.

300 ml whole milk

200 ml cream

1 vanilla pod

120 g sugar

3-5 grains of salt

7 pasteurised egg yolks

VANILLA ICECREAM

Add milk, cream, vanilla grains and the split pod, sugar and salt to a saucepan and bring to the boil (you need to add salt to break the sweetness and fat of the ice cream. Salt also helps bring out the vanilla taste).

Put the egg yolks in a bowl and carefully whisk in the warm cream. Then pour the custard back into the saucepan and place it over the heat again, warming it until it reaches approx. 84–85° C while whisking thoroughly. Remove the pan from the heat once the custard starts to thicken – if the custard becomes too hot it will curdle and turn into scrambled eggs!

Leave the custard to infuse for 10–15 minutes, by leaving the vanilla pod in the saucepan. Then sieve it back into a bowl and place it in the fridge. Stir it from time to time until it's cold.

Cool the custard in an ice cream machine until firm and creamy, and then freeze it until use. The ice cream will retain its creamy texture for 1–2 days, which is the best time to eat it.

Baked cauliflower with crab claws, junket dressing, green oil and flowers 148 · Crab salad with asparagus, dill, radish and toasted rye bread 151 · Boiled crab claws with grilled bread and tarragon cream 152 · Pasta with crab meat, ricotta, black pepper and parmesan 155

CRAB CLAWS

BAKED CAULIFLOWER

WITH CRAB CLAWS, JUNKET DRESSING, GREEN OIL AND FLOWERS

4–6 PEOPLE

1 cauliflower

2 tbsp. olive oil

2 tbsp. cider vinegar

salt and freshly ground pepper

500 g crab claws (boiled and prepared
    as described on page 152)

2 handfuls edible flowers
    (geranium, wood sorrel, thyme)

200 ml junket (now widely available
    in supermarkets, but if not, use
    natural Greek yoghurt or Icelandic
    Skyr, also widely available)

1 unwaxed lemon

1 tbsp. liquid honey

salt and freshly ground pepper

1 bunch flat leaved parsley

200 ml olive oil

1 clove garlic

salt and freshly ground pepper

Leave the nicer looking leaves on the cauliflower and remove the rest. Place the cauliflower in an ovenproof dish and drizzle olive oil and vinegar on top before sprinkling with salt and freshly ground pepper. Place the dish in the oven and bake for 20–25 minutes at 180° C, until its surface is beautifully golden and the cauliflower is tender, though not without bite. Take the cauliflower from the oven and place it in another dish before chopping it into big chunks.

Spread crab meat, junket dressing, green oil and flowers across the cauliflower chunks and serve the dish while still warm, as a lunch dish, part of a tasting menu or on a buffet.

JUNKET DRESSING

Pour the junket into a bowl and add lemon zest and juice, honey salt and freshly ground pepper before mixing until a smooth dressing. Leave the dressing to marinate for 10–15 minutes before serving it on top of the cauliflower.

GREEN OIL

Rinse the parsley and allow it to drip dry before putting it in a blender with oil, peeled garlic clove, salt and freshly ground pepper. Blend until it becomes a smooth, green oil.

CRAB SALAD

WITH ASPARAGUS, DILL, RADISH AND TOASTED RYE BREAD

4 PEOPLE

300 g crabmeat
   (approx. 1 kg crab claws, boiled
   as described on page 152)
10 green asparagus
1 bunch radishes
3–4 tbsp. olive oil
1 unwaxed lemon
salt and freshly ground pepper
1 bunch dill

Snap off the ends of the asparagus and rinse them in cold water. Then slice them finely and place them in a bowl with the fresh crabmeat.

Top and tail the radishes and rinse in cold water before slicing them finely. Add them to the bowl with crabmeat and asparagus.

Add olive oil, lemon zest and juice, salt and freshly ground pepper to taste and toss well. Chop the dill and sprinkle on top. Add more lemon, salt and freshly ground pepper if needed.

Serve the salad with toasted rye bread as a small lunch dish or a light summer dish.

BOILED CRAB CLAWS

WITH GRILLED BREAD AND TARRAGON CREAM

4 PEOPLE

———

1 kg crab claws

1 tbsp. sea salt

1 unwaxed lemon

10 whole black peppercorns

½ bunch dill

a few slices of bread

100 ml homemade mayonnaise

200 ml natural yoghurt

1 bunch tarragon

salt and freshly ground pepper

½ unwaxed lemon

8–12 bread slices

2 tbsp. olive oil

Place the crab claws in a saucepan and cover with water. Then add 1 tbsp. sea salt, 2 lemon slices, whole peppercorns and dill sprigs. Bring the claws to the boil and let them boil for 5–7 minutes. Then turn off the heat and leave them in the brine for approx. 20 minutes. Once the claws are cool, you bash them lightly with a hammer and remove the meat with a fork.

Drizzle olive oil on some bread slices and grill them on a hot grill pan or in the oven until completely golden and crispy.

You can also serve the crab claws whole and allow your guests to dig out the meat by themselves. Serve with tarragon cream and grilled bread.

TARRAGON CREAM

Add mayonnaise, yoghurt, salt and freshly ground pepper, lemon zest and juice to a blender and blend until it becomes a smooth green cream. Add lemon juice if needed and serve with the boiled crab claws.

PASTA

WITH CRABMEAT, RICOTTA, BLACK PEPPER AND PARMESAN

4 PEOPLE

100 ml milk

50 g ricotta

salt and freshly ground pepper

300 g crabmeat
   (approx. 1 kg crab claws as
   described on page 152)

300 g pasta
   (pappadelle, spaghetti, linguine)

50 g fresh Parmesan

Heat the milk in a small saucepan. Then take the pan off the heat and mix in ricotta until the two form a smooth cream. Add salt and freshly ground pepper to taste.

Bring a large saucepan with salt water to the boil and cook the pasta al dente before draining the water and tossing the pasta with the ricotta cream, crabmeat and grated Parmesan.

Serve the pasta right away with grated Parmesan and freshly ground pepper on top. It's a very simple and easy-to-make pasta dish that can be served for lunch or dinner.

TURBOT

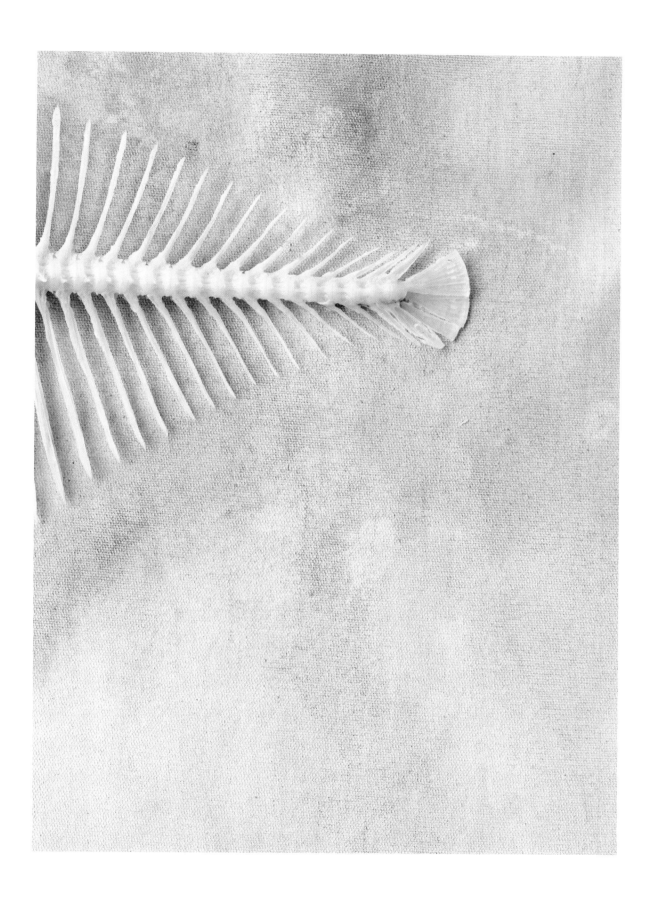

Turbot ceviche with coriander and fried flatbread

TURBOT CEVICHE

WITH CORIANDER AND FRIED FLATBREAD

4 PEOPLE

1 unwaxed lime

1 unwaxed lemon

¼ fresh red chilli without seeds

3 tbsp. good olive oil

sea salt and freshly ground pepper

200 g turbot fillet

1 bunch coriander

Add lime and lemon zest and juice to a bowl with finely chopped chilli, olive oil, salt and pepper and mix until a smooth dressing.

Finely slice the turbot fillet into strips of approx. ½ cm and add them to bowl with the dressing and toss well. Then leave the fish to marinate for a few minutes until it looks 'boiled' white on the outside.

Coarsely chop the coriander and toss well with the ceviche. Serve the dish right away. You may add a little salt and freshly ground pepper to taste. Serve the dish as a small starter or as part of a tasting menu with fried flatbread.

110 g yeast

200 ml lukewarm water

100 ml dark beer

300 g wheat flour

8 g sea salt

100 g wholegrain spelt flour
   or wholegrain Öland-wheat flour

100 ml olive oil for frying

sea salt

FRIED FLATBREAD

Dissolve the yeast in water and beer and then add a little wheat flour before adding salt, as the salt may otherwise 'kill' some of the yeast cells. Then add the rest of the flour and knead well until the dough is soft and smooth. Knead it well by lifting the dough with a wooden ladle until it comes away easily from the side of the bowl. Let the dough to rise in the bowl for approx. 1 hour, until it's doubled in size.

Then pull the dough from the bowl with your hands onto a flour-sprinkled kitchen top. Divide the dough into 8–10 lumps and pull or roll the lumps into thin flatbreads (much like pancakes). Fry them in some olive oil on a very hot pan for 1–2 minutes on each side, until crisp and golden. Then sprinkle with sea salt when they're all done and still warm. Serve with ceviche.

FRIED TURBOT

WITH GOOSEBERRIES, PEAS, MINT AND BROCCOLI

4 PEOPLE

600 g turbot fillet

1 broccoli

200 g fresh peas (without pods)

25 g butter

sea salt and freshly ground pepper

100 g fresh gooseberries

½ bunch mint

1 unwaxed lemon

2 tbsp. rapeseed oil

Divide the turbot fillet into 8 pieces and place the pieces on a dish. Sprinkle with a little salt and leave for 10-15 minutes.

Divide the broccoli into small pieces and rinse in cold water. Peel off the outer layer of the stalk and then slice it (approx. 1–2 cm).

Place broccoli and peas in a wide shallow saucepan and add 50 ml water, butter, a little salt and freshly ground pepper. Bring to the boil and let it boil for 1–2 minutes, to make sure the broccoli and peas are just cooked but retain their crispness and freshness. Add the halved gooseberries, the coarsely chopped mint as well as lemon zest and juice.

Heat a pan and fry the turbot in a little oil over high heat for approx. 1 minute each side until the pieces are nicely golden on the outside yet succulent in the middle.

Remove the turbot from the pan and sprinkle with salt and freshly ground pepper before serving on a plate or in a dish. Add broccoli and peas and use the liquid from their pan as a sauce. Then garnish with some fresh mint leaves and serve the turbot right away with good bread and possibly a green salad.

TURBOT BISQUE

WITH CHARRED TOMATOES AND CHERVIL

4 PEOPLE

1 kg turbot bones

100 ml olive oil

200 ml white wine

1 leek

1 fennel

5 thyme sprigs

1 clove garlic

8-10 whole peppercorns

1–1½ litre water

100 ml cream

1 unwaxed lemon

salt and freshly ground pepper

16-20 small tomatoes

1 pot chervil

Chop the turbot bones into smaller bits and rinse them well in cold water to make sure that no blood or intestines are left. Dry them well.

Heat a thick-bottomed saucepan and add 2 tbsp. olive oil. Braise the turbot bones until nicely coloured. Then add white wine, finely chopped leek, fennel, thyme, garlic and peppercorns and leave to sauté for a few minutes. Then add water to just cover the bones and bring to the boil before turning the heat right down and leaving it to simmer for 15–20 minutes. Skim the froth to get rid of impurities.

After 15–20 minutes, switch off the heat and leave the broth to steep for another 15 minutes. Then sieve the broth through a finely meshed sieve into a clean saucepan. Bring the broth to the boil again and reduce to half. Then add cream, lemon zest and juice, salt and freshly ground pepper to taste.

Heat a frying pan and add the tomatoes. Let them char nicely on a dry pan for approx. 2 minutes on each side.

Place 3–4 tomatoes in a deep dish or a bowl and pour the warm bisque on top. Garnish with chervil and drizzle a few drops of olive oil on top. Serve immediately with good bread.

Braised whole turbot with thyme, garlic and fennel

BRAISED WHOLE TURBOT

WTH THYME, GARLIC AND FENNEL

4–6 PEOPLE

1 whole turbot, 2½ – 3 kg

2 fennel bulbs

3 cloves garlic

½ bunch thyme

salt and freshly ground pepper

1 unwaxed lemon

300 ml white wine

20 g butter

50 ml cold-pressed olive oil

1 pot garden nasturtium

½ bunch tarragon

Rinse the turbot thoroughly, dry it off and place in a large roasting pan. Add 1 finely sliced fennel, coarsely chopped garlic and thyme, salt and freshly ground pepper, lemon slices and white wine before covering the pan with foil and putting it in a pre-heated oven. Bake the turbot for 25-30 minutes at 160° C.

Take the turbot from the oven, drain the liquid into a saucepan, and heat to reduce to half. Let the turbot rest for 10 minutes before scraping off the skin and removing the fillets (big pieces if possible).

Dice the butter and whisk into the reduced broth to thicken it. Carefully heat the sauce and add olive oil and possibly a little more salt and freshly ground pepper as well as lemon juice to taste.

Finely slice half of the remaining fennel on a mandolin and finely dice the other half. Add diced fennel, a little chopped tarragon and garden nasturtiums to the warm sauce.

Serve the turbot fillets on a plate or a dish and pour the warm sauce on top before garnishing with fennel slices and chopped herbs. Serve right away with good bread to soak up the sauce.

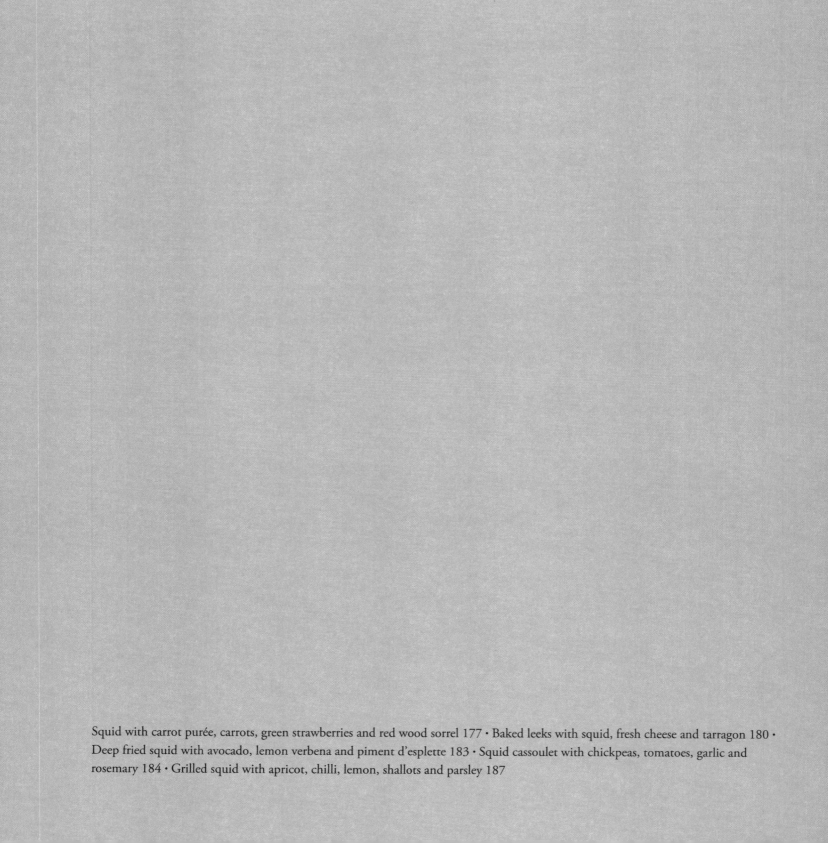

SQUID

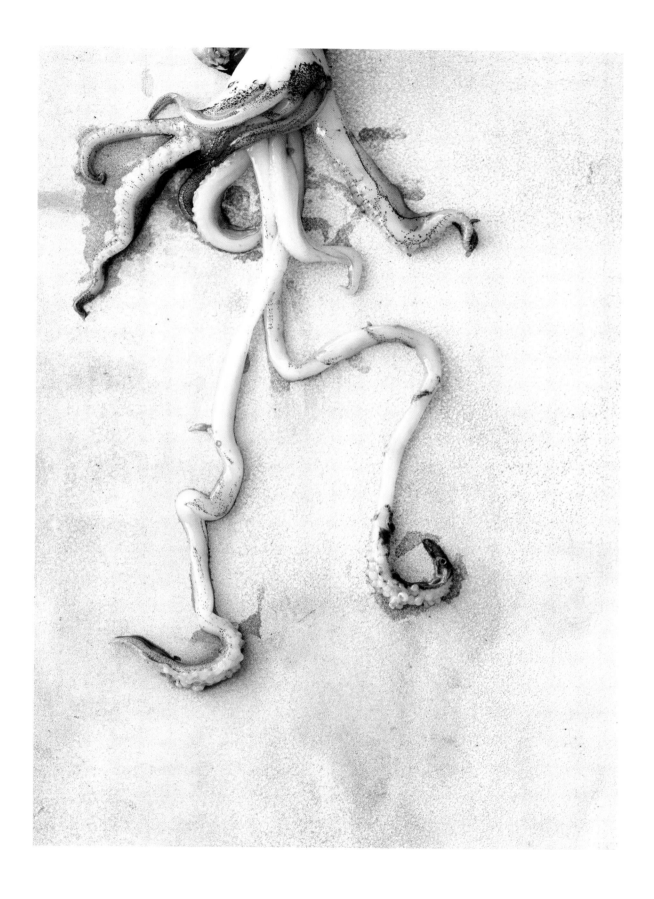

SQUID

WITH CARROT PURÉE, CARROT, GREEN STRAWBERRIES AND RED WOOD SORREL

4 PEOPLE

500 g fresh squid
2-3 tbsp. olive oil
1 clove garlic
4 small new carrots
4-6 green strawberries
salt and freshly ground pepper
1 handful red wood sorrel

4 large carrots
50 ml cold-pressed olive oil
1 unwaxed lemon
1 tbsp. liquid honey
sea salt and freshly ground pepper

Clean the squid and rise thoroughly in cold water. You can also ask your fishmonger to do this for you. Finely slice the squid and place the squid rings in a bowl. Then marinate them in a little olive oil and chopped garlic.

Rinse the carrots and remove most of the top but leave a little. Finely slice them lengthways on a mandolin or with a vegetable peeler. Place the carrot strips in a bowl with cold water to keep them crisp. Finely slice the green strawberries.

Fry the squid rings in a hot pan for ½–1 minute. Don't fry them all at once as this will draw the heat from the pan and squid should be fried quickly over great heat. If the temperature is too low, the squid will start to boil and become tough and hard. Remove the last squid rings from the pan and sprinkle all of them with salt and freshly ground pepper to taste.

Place the warm carrot purée in the bottom of a deep dish and place the fried squid on top and then garnish with carrot strips and green strawberries. Finally, drizzle a little olive oil on top. Serve the dish at once as a starter or as part of a tasting menu.

CARROT PURÉE

Peel the carrots and chop them before boiling them for approx. 20 minutes, until tender. Drain the water and place the carrots in a blender. Add olive oil, lemon zest and juice, honey, salt and freshly ground pepper and blend until a smooth purée. Possibly add a little more lemon to ensure that the taste is very fresh.

Baked leek with squid, fresh cream cheese and tarragon

BAKED LEEK

WITH SQUID, FRESH CREAM CHEESE AND TARRAGON

4 PEOPLE

500 g fresh squid

1 tbsp. olive oil

1 clove garlic

50 g fresh cream cheese

1 unwaxed lemon

salt and freshly ground pepper

2 tbsp. olive oil

1 bunch tarragon

Clean the squid and rinse thoroughly in cold water. You can also ask your fishmonger to do this. Finely slice the squid and place the squid rings in a bowl. Then marinate them in 1 tbsp. olive oil and chopped garlic for 30 minutes.

Whisk the fresh cream cheese with lemon zest and juice, salt and freshly ground pepper and 2 tbsp. olive oil until smooth.

Fry the squid rings on a hot pan for ½–1 minute. Don't fry them all at once as this will draw the heat from the pan and squid should be fried quickly over great heat. If the temperature is too low, the squid will start to boil and thus become tough and hard. Remove the last squid rings from the pan and sprinkle all of them with salt and freshly ground pepper to taste.

Serve the squid rings on top of baked leeks garnished with fresh cream cheese mixture and tarragon.

4 medium-sized leeks
3 tbsp. olive oil
sea salt

BAKED LEEKS

Top and tail the leeks and split them lengthways before rinsing them in cold water. You can soak them in cold water to make sure that there's no dirt left. Then remove the leeks from the water and let them drip dry.

Place the leeks in a roasting pan covered in baking paper and drizzle olive oil on top before sprinkling with sea salt. Bake the leeks for 30–40 minutes at 180° C until they become nicely charred and tender. This will bring out their sweetness and rid them of their tanginess while intensifying the leek-taste itself.

Tip

You can easily prepare the leeks 1–2 days in advance and then just heat them right before use or serve them cold.

DEEP FRIED SQUID

WITH AVOCADO, LEMON VERBENA AND PIMENT D'ESPLETTE

4 PEOPLE

500 g fresh squid

1 egg

100 g panko or fine breadcrumbs

1 litre rapeseed oil

salt

2 avocados

1 unwaxed lemon

2 tbsp. olive oil

1 tbsp. Piment d'Esplette (these fiery
   red peppers can be found in dried or
   powdered form from most delicatessens.
   If not, then hot paprika can be used).

1 pot verbena

a little bronze fennel

Clean the squid and rinse thoroughly in cold water. You can also ask your fishmonger to do this. Finely slice the body and chop the arms into smaller pieces.

Whisk the egg and then toss the squid first in egg mixture then in breadcrumbs. Make sure that they're evenly covered. Heat the rapeseed oil in a small saucepan until 160° C.

Split the avocados and remove the stone before slicing the avocado flesh. Place the slices on 4 plates and drizzle with lemon juice, olive oil, salt and Piment d'Esplette.

Carefully lower the bread-crumbed squid in the hot oil and deep fry for 1–2 minutes until crispy and golden on the outside while remaining succulent in the middle. Remove the crisp squid from the oil and place the pieces on kitchen towels. Then sprinkle with salt before placing them on top of the avocado slices. Garnish with verbena, bronze fennel and Piment d'Esplette.

Serve the deep fried squid straight away while they're still warm and crispy. Serve as a lunch dish or a starter.

SQUID 'CASSOULET'

WITH CHICKPEAS, TOMATO, GARLIC AND ROSEMARY

4 PEOPLE

300 g soaked chickpeas

1 onion

2 cloves garlic

4 tbsp. olive oil

2 rosemary sprigs

3-4 ripe tomatoes

salt and freshly ground pepper

500 g squid

1 unwaxed lemon

Clean the squid and rinse in cold water. Coarsely chop the squid and marinate the pieces in a little rosemary, garlic and olive oil.

Boil the chickpeas in water for 35–40 minutes, until tender but not without a little bite. Remove the pot from the heat and drain excess water.

Peel the onion and cloves of garlic and chop finely. Add 2 tbsp. oil, onion, 1 rosemary sprig and garlic to a pot and sauté for a couple of minutes, so that the onion remains translucent. Don't let it brown. Add chickpeas and leave to sauté for another couple of minutes.

Dice the tomatoes and add them to the pot with chickpeas and let everything simmer for 10–15 minutes, until the tomatoes release their liquid and collapse and it becomes a dense 'cassoulet'. Add salt and freshly ground pepper to taste.

Fry the squid on a hot pan for ½–1 minute. Don't fry all the pieces at once, as this will draw the heat from the pan and squid should be fried quickly over great heat. If the temperature is too low, the squid will start to boil and thus become tough and hard. Remove the last squid rings from the pan and sprinkle all of them with salt and freshly ground pepper to taste.

Toss the squid with the chickpeas and add salt and freshly ground pepper, lemon zest and juice to taste. Serve the cassoulet with good bread.

GRILLED SQUID

WITH APRICOT, CHILLI, LEMON, SHALLOTS AND PARSLEY

4 PEOPLE

500 g fresh squid

1 tbsp. olive oil

4 fresh apricots

½ fresh red chilli

2 shallots

1 bunch flat leaved parsley

50 ml olive oil

1 unwaxed lemon

salt and freshly ground pepper

Clean the squid and rinse thoroughly in cold water. You can also ask your fishmonger to do this. Chop both body and arms. And marinate the pieces in a little olive oil for 10–15 minutes.

Halve the apricots and remove the stone before cutting the meat into thin wedges. Finely chop chilli, shallots and parsley and mix in a bowl with the apricots. Add oil, lemon zest and juice, salt and freshly ground pepper and toss until it becomes thick vinaigrette.

Grill the squid on a very hot grill pan for approx. 30 seconds on both sides, charring them nicely without overcooking them. Remove the squid from the pan and sprinkle with salt and freshly ground pepper.

Place the squid on a dish and cover with vinaigrette. Serve while the squid is still warm as a starter or lunch dish.

RAZOR
CLAMS

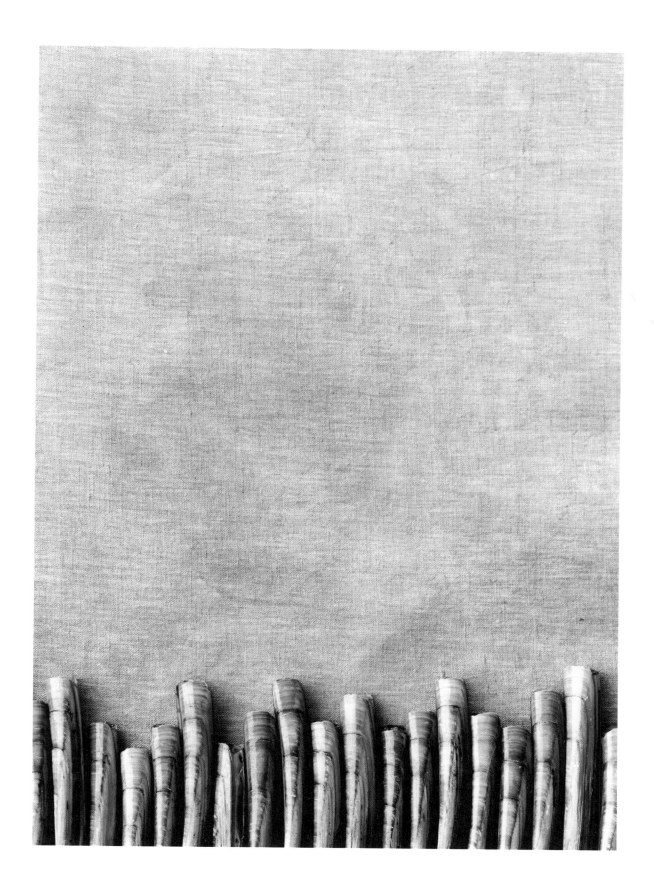

GRILLED CABBAGE

WITH RAZOR CLAM BLANQUETTE AND SWEET CICELY

4 PEOPLE

1 pointed cabbage

1 kg razor clams

2 shallots

1 clove garlic

50 ml olive oil

200 ml white wine

5 thyme sprigs

25-35 g butter

1 bunch sweet cicely
    (if you can't find sweet cicely,
    use chervil, tarragon or parsley
    as substitutes)

salt and freshly ground pepper

1 unwaxed lemon

Remove damaged outer leaves from the head of the pointed cabbage before cutting it into eight wedges lengthways. Rinse well in cold water.

Rinse the razor clams thoroughly in cold water to remove sand and other impurities.

Peel shallots and garlic and chop finely. Add to a saucepan with 2 tbsp. olive oil and sauté for 1-2 minutes, until tender but not brown.

Add the clams to the pan and then add white wine and thyme before covering with a lid. Steam the clams for 2–3 minutes until they open. Take the saucepan off the heat and remove the clams from their shells. Save the liquid, pour into a clean saucepan and simmer to reduce by half.

Once reduced, whisk the cold butter bit by bit into the warm mussel broth to thicken it, until it becomes creamy like a blanquette. Do not allow it to boil once you've added butter.

Chop the razor clams into smaller pieces and add them to the blanquette. Add lots of chopped sweet cicely and then salt and freshly ground pepper to taste.

Allow the cabbage to drip dry and toss with a little olive oil and finely grated lemon zest. Fry the cabbage on a hot grill pan or an ordinary frying pan for 1–2 minutes on each side. The cabbage should be well charred on the outside and still crispy in the middle. Remove the cabbage from the heat and add salt and freshly ground pepper to taste before serving it on a plate smothered in the warm razor shell blanquette. Garnish with lots of sweet cicely.

PASTA

WITH RAZOR CLAMS, KALE, RICOTTA AND ALMONDS

4 PEOPLE

---

500 g razor clams

1 shallot

1 clove garlic

50 ml olive oil

100 ml white wine

50 g ricotta

300 g penne

100 plucked and cleaned kale

25 g almonds

40 g fresh Parmesan

1 unwaxed lemon

salt and freshly ground pepper

Rinse the razor clams thoroughly in cold water to remove sand and other impurities.

Peel shallots and garlic and chop finely. Add to a pot with 2 tbsp. olive oil and sauté for 1–2 minutes, until tender but not brown.

Add the razor clams before adding white wine and covering with a lid. Steam the mussels for 2–3 minutes, until open. Take the pan off the heat and remove the clams from their shells. Sieve the liquid broth into another pan and let it cool. Stir ricotta into the razor clam broth to make a creamy sauce, then add the razor clam meat.

Pour water into a saucepan and add a little salt before bringing it to the boil. Add the pasta and let it boil for 7–8 minutes, until the pasta is al dente. Then drain the water from the pasta.

Toss the warm pasta with the creamy razor clam broth, coarsely chopped kale, chopped almonds, freshly grated Parmesan, lemon zest, salt and freshly ground pepper.

Serve the pasta in bowls or deep dishes with good bread as a main meal.

STEAMED RAZOR CLAMS

WITH HERBS AND TOMATOES

4 PEOPLE

1 kg razor clams
2 shallots
1 clove garlic
50 ml olive oil
15 small cherry or cocktail tomatoes
200 ml white wine
salt and freshly ground pepper
2 large handfuls herbs
   (sweet cicely, bronze fennel,
   chervil, parsley or whatever else
   you have)

Rinse the razor clams thoroughly in cold water to remove sand and other impurities.

Peel shallots and garlic and chop finely. Add to a saucepan with 2 tbsp. olive oil and sauté for 1–2 minutes, until tender but not browning.

Halve the tomatoes and add them to the saucepan before adding razor clams and white wine. Cover with a lid and steam the mussels for 2–3 minutes, until open.

Toss it all well and add salt and freshly ground pepper to taste before sprinkling with lots of coarsely chopped herbs and finally drizzling a little olive oil on top. Serve the clams straight away with good bread to soak up the wonderful broth.

RAZOR CLAM BROTH

WITH PEAS AND ORPINE

4 PEOPLE

1 kg razor clams

2 shallots

1 clove garlic

50 ml olive oil

200 ml white wine

5 thyme sprigs

100 ml cream

100 g peas without pods

12-16 tiny baby orpine leaves
  (you can use parsley or tarragon
  for the same taste, with a few fava
  or green beans to get the same
  crunch as orpine)

1 unwaxed lemon

salt and freshly ground pepper

Rinse the razor clams thoroughly in cold water to remove sand and other impurities.

Peel shallots and garlic and chop finely. Add to a saucepan with 2 tbsp. olive oil and sauté for 1–2 minutes, until tender but not browned.

Add the shells to the saucepan and then white wine and thyme before covering with a lid. Steam the mussels for 2-3 minutes until they open. Take the pan off the heat and take the meat from the shells.

Sieve the liquid into another pan and add cream before bringing to the boil for a few minutes. Do not reduce the broth too much but allow it to maintain its fresh, lovely taste of clams. Whisk the broth thoroughly with a mixer or hand blender until it becomes wonderfully frothy

Serve the clams in bowls or deep dishes with peas and orpine leaves. Add lemon zest and juice, salt and freshly ground pepper to taste before pouring the broth over the mussels. Finally, drizzle a little olive oil on top and serve immediately with good bread.

Orpine: A purple-flowered Eurasian plant of the stonecrop family, a naturalized weed of North America now growing happily all over the European continent as well.

Razor clams with dill, kohlrabi and cucumber

RAZOR CLAMS

WITH DILL, KOHLRABI AND CUCUMBER

4 PEOPLE

1 kg razor clams

2 shallots

1 clove garlic

50 ml olive oil

200 ml white wine

5 thyme sprigs

Rinse the razor clams thoroughly in cold water to remove sand and other impurities.

Peel shallots and garlic and chop finely. Add to a saucepan with 2 tbsp. olive oil and sauté for 1-2 minutes, until tender but not browned.

Add the shells to the pan and then white wine and thyme before covering with a lid. Steam the shells for 2-3 minutes until they open. Take the pan off the heat and take the mussels from the shells. Drain the liquid into a bag and freeze it to use, as excellent fish stock, at another time.

Serve the kohlrabi and cucumber on a dish or plate with razor clams 'wedged' in between (see image on previous page). Then drizzle with buttermilk dressing and dill oil on the top and around the sides. Add salt and freshly ground pepper to taste and finally, garnish with a little dill and tarragon.

Serve the razor clams immediately, while the kohlrabi and cucumber are still completely fresh and crispy. Serve with good bread as a starter, as part of a tasting menu or as a side dish with fish.

1 bunch dill

salt and freshly ground pepper

1 kohlrabi

1 cucumber

200 ml buttermilk

1 tbsp. liquid honey

1 unwaxed lemon

½ bunch tarragon

DILL OIL, KOHLRABI, CUCUMBER AND BUTTERMILK DRESSING

Place the dill (save a little as garnish), olive oil, salt and freshly ground pepper in blender and blend until it becomes smooth, green oil. Then pour the oil into a bowl ready to use in the final assembly of the dish.

Peel kohlrabi and cucumber and finely slice both on a mandolin. Then put them in another bowl ready to use with the razor clams (see left)

Mix buttermilk, honey, lemon zest and juice as well as salt and freshly ground pepper. Let the dressing marinate for 15–20 minutes to thicken before using as the third component of the final assembly.

ZANDER

(ALSO KNOWN AS PIKE-PERCH)

ZANDER SALAD

WITH CAPERS, PARSLEY ROOT, FENNEL, DILL AND PARSLEY ON GRILLED BREAD

4 PEOPLE

400 g zander fillet

salt and freshly ground pepper

50 ml olive oil

3 parsley roots

1 fennel bulb

300 ml natural yoghurt

1 tbsp. mustard

1 tsp. liquid honey

2 tbsp. capers

½ bunch dill

½ bunch flat leaved parsley

4–8 slices good wheat bread

Place the zander fillets in an ovenproof dish and sprinkle with salt and freshly ground pepper to taste before drizzling a little olive oil on top. Bake the fillets for 7-8 minutes at 120° C in a preheated oven. Make sure they're just done and still succulent in the middle. Take them out of the oven and let them cool.

Finely dice two parsley roots and place them in a bowl with yoghurt, mustard, honey, salt and freshly ground pepper and mix into a good dressing.

Finely dice half the fennel and coarsely chop 2 tbsp. capers before adding both to the dressing. Finely slice the remaining half fennel and the last parsley root (use a mandolin) and place the slices in a bowl with cold water to keep them crisp.

Divide the zander fillets into smaller pieces and toss in the dressing. Rinse dill and parsley and let them drip dry before chopping. Save a little of the herbs as garnish. Add the chopped herbs to the salad and add salt and freshly ground pepper to taste.

Dip the bread slices in olive oil and grill them on a hot grill pan or in the oven until golden and crisp. Serve the salad with the slices of crisp bread as a lunch dish or a starter.

FRIED ZANDER

WITH BOLETUS EDILUS, NORTH SEA CHEESE, TARRAGON AND WOOD SORREL

4 PEOPLE

1 whole zander of approx. 1½ kg
   in weight or 800 g zander fillet
400 g boletus edilus
or other wild mushrooms
2 tbsp. olive oil
10 g butter
salt and freshly ground pepper
25 g North Sea cheese (use Gouda
   or Comte as substitutes)
   a handful of tarragon and
   wood sorrel

Fillet the zander or ask your fishmonger to do it for you. Divide the fillets into four equal pieces and place them on a dish. Sprinkle with a little salt and let the zander marinate for 30 minutes.

Clean the boletus edilus with a small knife and cut them into smaller pieces. Fry the mushrooms on a hot frying pan with a little oil for a few minutes until they get a lovely crust. Then add butter to the pan and allow it to sizzle around the mushrooms. Add salt and freshly ground pepper to taste.

Place the mushrooms in a bowl and wipe the frying pan clean before adding a little oil. Fry the zander fillets at medium heat for approx. 2 minutes on one side, to give them a wonderfully golden crust. Then turn the fillets over on the other side and fry for another 30 seconds so that the fillets are just done and still succulent in the middle.

Serve the crisp zander fillets with the mushrooms, grated cheese and herbs on top as a lunch dish or with good bread as a main dish.

Tartar of zander with kohlrabi, junket, marigolds and cress

TARTAR OF ZANDER

WITH KOHLRABI, JUNKET, MARIGOLDS AND CRESS

4 PEOPLE

150 g zander fillet
salt and freshly ground pepper
1 kohlrabi
50 ml junket (or Greek
   yoghurt or Skyr)
½ unwaxed lemon
1 tsp. liquid honey
2 tbsp. buckwheat
2 marigolds or any other
   edible flower
1 pot cress

Make sure the zander fillet is fresh. It's very important that it's completely fresh when serving it raw. Finely dice the zander fillet. Use a very sharp knife to ensure that you cut the meat rather than mashing it. Place the diced fish in a bowl and add salt and freshly ground pepper to taste.

Peel the kohlrabi before finely slicing it on a mandolin. Mix junket with lemon zest and juice, honey, salt and freshly ground pepper.

Fry the buckwheat on a dry pan until it starts popping and giving off scent. Remove the pan from the heat and leave to cool.

Serve the zander tartar in kohlrabi slices (like a small taco) and drizzle with junket dressing before garnishing with buckwheat, marigolds and cress.

Serve the zander tartar as a canape with a glass of champagne or a welcome drink. You can also serve it as a small starter in a tasting menu.

ZANDER FISHCAKES

WITH MARINATED SUMMER GREENS

4 PEOPLE

600 g zander fillet

1 tsp. salt

2 eggs

2 tbsp. wheat flour

150 ml whole milk

1 carrot

1 baking potato

½ bunch dill

freshly ground pepper

10 g butter

1 tbsp. rapeseed oil for frying

2 tbsp. coarse mustard

100 ml cider vinegar

50 ml sugar

2 garden carrots

1 fennel bulb

½ cauliflower

salt and freshly ground pepper

Coarsely mince the zander fillet in a meat grinder (or possibly a food processor). Place the minced fish in a bowl and mix in salt. Mixing the fish with salt enables it to bind liquids and not separate. Add eggs, flour and whole milk a little at a time and mix well until the mixture has a suitable consistency.

Peel the carrot and potato and finely grate both. Squeeze the liquid from the vegetables and mix in with the minced fish. Finally, add chopped dill and pepper and let the mixture rest for approx. 30 minutes in the fridge.

After 30 minutes, take the mixture out and shape small handfuls into patties about the size of your palm. Fry the zander fishcakes at medium-heat in half butter, half oil for 1–2 minutes on each side, to give them a nice crust while remaining succulent in the middle.

Serve the warm zander fishcakes with marinated summer greens and good rye bread.

MARINATED SUMMER GREENS

Add mustard, vinegar and sugar to a saucepan and bring to the boil, then remove the pan from the heat.

Finely slice the carrots, fennel and cauliflower and add the vegetables to the warm vinegar pickle and toss well. Leave the vegetables to marinate for 15-20 minutes before serving them with the zander fishcakes.

Tip: You can easily make a large portion of the summer greens and then keep them in a jar in the fridge or cellar if you have one.

Grilled zander with creamed potato and a garnish of crisp potato, watercress and chicken skin

GRILLED ZANDER

WITH CREAMED POTATO AND A GARNISH OF CRISP POTATO, WATERCRESS AND CHICKEN SKIN

4 PEOPLE

600 g zander fillet

salt and freshly ground pepper

800 g potatoes, egg size

1 litre grape seed oil

2 chicken breast skins
(you can leave this out or
substitute with 2 bacon slices)

150 g butter

100 ml whole milk

1 tbsp. olive oil

a little watercress

Make sure the zander fillet is fresh and then divide the fillet into four pieces. Sprinkle with a little salt and place in the fridge.

Peel the potatoes and dice all but two. Finely slice 2 potatoes on a mandolin and place them in a bowl with cold water. Add the remaining potatoes to a saucepan and cover with water. Bring the potatoes to the boil and let them boil for 15-20 minutes, until tender.

Heat the oil in another saucepan, while the potatoes are boiling. Drip-dry the potato slices before deep-frying them in hot oil for 1–2 minutes, until golden and crisp.

Place the chicken skins on a baking sheet with baking paper and sprinkle with salt before placing them in the oven. Bake the chicken skin for 8-10 minutes at 180° C, until golden and crisp. Remove the skins from the oven and place them on a piece of kitchen towel to allow excess fat to drip off.

Add butter and milk to a saucepan and heat until the butter has melted. Drain the potatoes and mash them with a potato masher or a whisk and add hot milk and butter until they becomes soft and creamy. Keep the mash warm in its saucepan.

Drizzle the zander fillets with a little olive oil and cook carefully on a hot grill pan or barbecue for approx. 2 minutes on one side. Then turn the fillets over and cook for another 30 seconds on the other side.

Take the zander fillets off the heat. Serve them on top of the mashed potato, sprinkled with lightly crushed chicken skin and potato crisps. Finally, garnish with a little watercress and serve immediately while both fish and potato are still warm.

ON THE

BEACH

STEAMED MUSSELS
ON THE BEACH

WITH BEER AND BEACH HERBS

4 PEOPLE

1 – 1½ kg mussels (this is about 40 mussels)

1 shallot

1 clove garlic

½ fennel bulb

2 tbsp. olive oil

2 handfuls wild (beach) herbs

5 thyme sprigs

1 can or bottle of beer

1 Primus stove

Rinse the mussels thoroughly in cold water to remove all sand. Peel shallot and garlic and finely chop. Finely chop fennel as well.

Light your primus and place a large saucepan on top. Add oil and half the wild beach herbs and sauté for 1-2 minutes, until tender, without browning. Remove the herbs from the pan.

Add thyme and mussels to the pot. Then add beer and steam the mussels under a lid for 3-5 minutes, until they open (discard the ones that don't open). Put the herbs back into the pot and toss well.

Take the pot off the heat and garnish with the remaining half of the beach herbs. Serve the mussels right away with some of the broth and good bread.

Tip: What are beach herbs? These are salt tolerant edibles, such as yarrow, mint, purslane and sea sandwort (see langoustine recipe on p96) If you can't find any beach herbs, you can easily substitute them with flat leaved parsley, chervil or tarragon.

APPLE-CINNAMON CAKE (To bring with you)

12–16 PIECES

150 g soft butter

150 g sugar

150 g marzipan

150 g eggs

2–3 tbsp. flour

1 unwaxed lemon

2–3 apples
   (Ingrid Marie, Discovery or
   Red Aroma)

1 tbsp. cinnamon

1 tbsp. cane sugar

Mix butter, sugar and marzipan until soft. Then add eggs a little at a time until it becomes like cake batter. Then stir in flour and lemon zest.

Grease a cake tin with a little butter and pour in the cake batter. Finely slice the apples and sprinkle them with a little cane sugar and cinnamon before spreading them on top of the batter.

Place the cake in the oven and bake for 30–35 minutes at 170° C, until beautifully golden on top and firm in the middle.

Remove the cake from the oven and leave it to cool before slicing and serving it. You an easily bake this cake the day before use, as it maintains both moisture and freshness well.

HOT ELDERBERRY SYRUP (To bring with you)

WITH LEMON AND CANE SUGAR

20-25 CUPS

500 g fresh elderberries
  (or frozen)
2 litres water
300 g cane sugar
2 star anises
1 apple, diced
2 unwaxed lemons

Place the elderberries in a saucepan with water, sugar, star anise, apple and 1 sliced lemon. Bring everything to the boil and let the syrup boil for 10 minutes until the tastes of elderberry, apple and lemon are well integrated.

Remove the saucepan from the heat and let the syrup infuse for another 20-30 minutes on the kitchen table. Sieve the syrup into a clean saucepan and add a little fresh lemon juice to taste.

Heat the syrup and pour into a thermos to take on your mussel-foraging beach trip. You can drink the syrup warm or cold. It'll keep in the fridge for 2–3 weeks.

SEASONAL FISHING CALENDAR

	JAN	FEB	MAR	APR	MAY
PERCH	●	●	■	■	◆
SQUID	●	●	●	◆	◆
GARFISH*					◆
LANGOUSTINE	●	●	●	●	■
RAZOR CLAMS**	●	●	◆	◆	●
CRAYFISH FEMALE	▼	▼	▼	●	●
CRAYFISH MALE	▼	▼	▼	▼	▼
MACKEREL	●	●	●	◆	◆
MUSSELS**	●	●	◆	◆	●
TURBOT	●	●	◆	◆	■
RAY	●	●	●	●	■
PLAICE	●	◆	◆	■	■
EDIBLE CRAB	■	■	●	●	●
EEL***	●	●	●	●	▼

*GARFISH

You can only catch garfish in Northern European & Atlantic waters for a limited time.

**MUSSELS

Although the popular guideline states that you should only gather mussels (and oysters) in months containing an 'r', in principle, you can gather mussels all year round. Avoid hard frost, as mussels die when pulled out of the water. You should also be extra alert in the hot summer months, as there is risk of algae in the water.

	Season	◆ Peak Season	■ Spawning	▼ Protected		

JUN	JUL	AUG	SEP	OCT	NOV	DEC
◆	◆	◆	◆	●	●	●
◆	◆	■	■	■	●	●
●	●	◆	◆			
■	◆	◆	◆	◆	●	●
◆	●	●	◆	◆	◆	●
●	●	●	●	▼	▼	▼
▼	▼	●	●	▼	▼	▼
■	■	◆	◆	●	●	●
◆	●	●	◆	◆	◆	●
■	■	●	◆	◆	◆	●
■	■	◆	◆	◆	◆	●
■	◆	◆	◆	◆	◆	●
●	●	◆	◆	◆	◆	■
▼	▼	◆	◆	●	●	●

* * * E E L

Eels are not generally protected, however, there are rules
on which tools you may use to catch them and when, so
remember to always check up on this before you go fishing.

INDEX